Loving The Addict,
Hating The Addiction

Loving The Addict, Hating The Addiction

◆

For Christian families coping with drug addiction

Kecia C. Sims

iUniverse, Inc.

New York Lincoln Shanghai

Loving The Addict, Hating The Addiction
For Christian families coping with drug addiction

iUniverse, Inc.

For information address:
iUniverse, Inc.
2021 Pine Lake Road, Suite 100
Lincoln, NE 68512
www.iuniverse.com

All verses are quoted from the King James version of the bible unless otherwise noted.

ISBN: 0-595-28888-X (pbk)
ISBN: 0-595-65930-6 (cloth)

Printed in the United States of America

This book is dedicated to my beautiful and precious son, Jonathan, who was in the fire with me. I thank God for your love and strength. I'm glad that I taught you how to pray because there were many days your precious prayers gave me strength.

I know you saw, heard, and suffered a lot of painful things. But I pray that some day you will understand God's word in **Romans 8:28, "And we know that all things work together for good to them that love God, to them who are the called according to his purpose."**

Jonathan, God called you at a young age. Fulfill your purpose in life and you will go far. Stay with God and seek Him all the days of your life. All of the curses have been broken. You will be a mighty man of God.

I love you forever,

Mom

Produce your cause, saith the Lord; bring forth your strong reasons, saith the King of Jacob.

Isaiah 41:21

Contents

Acknowledgements

During the time I was coping with drug addiction in my home, I had endless love and support around me. Many times I felt lonely but I was never alone. My Lord and Savior Jesus Christ said He would never leave me nor forsake me and I'm so glad He honors His word. I thank God for protecting me and guiding me through the storm.

To my family, I love you all. You are awesome and unique! We are a big family full of love and support and that means the world to me. I could not have survived without you. I love you for being examples of faith and strength. You supported me during some of the craziest days of my life. Thank you for feeding us when we didn't have money for food. Thank you for understanding why I stayed in the fire as long as I did. I know that it wasn't easy to watch my process because I know when one of us is hurting, we all hurt. Again, I thank you for just being there. I pray that we continue to grow stronger in unity and love. Many forces have tried, but nothing can separate us! As long as we stay with God, not even death can keep us apart.

Mom, I want the world to know how much you mean to me. Thank you for teaching me how to be strong. Thank you for teaching me to look directly in a person's eyes when I talk to them. That trick has been invaluable! We've got much work to do together, so just be prepared. Remember, when I go up, you go up.

I am so thankful for grace and mercy, also known as my brothers, Jonathan and Patrick. During my ordeal I had to call on you guys a lot. I want you to know how much I appreciate you for coming to my rescue. It's amazing how holy men remain sanctified when they really want to do some serious "furniture movin'!"

Friends are very important to me. Paris, Greta, Katrina and Kesha, I love you all for being there for the past eighteen years (It's been over twenty years for you Greta). Paris, I love you for your gift of encouragement that God has placed in you. Don't ever stop letting God use you. Treasure that gift because it's always needed. Greta, girl we go way back! I love you for allowing me to talk your ears off. I know you felt my pain and I thank you for encouraging me to be strong. Katrina, I love you for keeping it real. You are the only person who still talks trash to me. These days, I am highly respected as the "preacher" or "evangelist" by a lot of people except you! You often remind me that you knew me before I got in the church or I should say before the church got in me. One day God told me that you were good for me just the way you are because you keep me humble. But you still need Jesus! Kesha, I thank you for your "speedy moving services." You are my hero! I also thank you for keeping my feet healthy and pretty! Your peppermint and citrus pedicures are the bomb!

Prayer is very important to me. The Lord has blessed me with some powerful sisters who know how to get a prayer through. Evangelist Carol, I thank God for you. It was your motivation that encouraged me to complete this book and I am eternally grateful. Evangelist Lanetta, I love you! Please keep the prayer wheel turning. Your prayers go past the ceiling and right to the throne of God. Thank you for allowing God to use you to be the calm in the midst of the storm. Your prayers have brought me through so much. Your calming presence and ministering prayers are the perfect prescription to prepare me to preach. Thank you for blessing me so I can be a blessing to God's people. Evangelist Inecir, I thank God for you taking the time to seek the Lord concerning me. It's wonderful to know when the Lord places someone on your heart, you carefully pray over the word you received from the Lord before delivering it. Keep seeking God regarding His people. You are a powerful tool to the Kingdom.

Dr. Lelia Edwards, I thank you for your wisdom. Thank you for telling me to step to the podium like a lady and then preach like I'm crazy. I will always do just that!

Dr. Betty Hendricks, thank you for praying for me over the years. Thank you for speaking into my life. I will stay on the wall!

The Lord has allowed me to make two very special "Divine Connections." The first was with Elder Vikki Johnson, Pastor of Women at Kingdom Worship Center in Towson, MD. Elder Vikki, although I have yet to meet you in person or even speak to you on the telephone, I thank God for you because you encouraged me to soar like an eagle. I have been soaring ever since. Our connection is an example of how the Internet should really be used! You gave me a word from the Lord via email and it is coming to pass. I look forward to doing great things together in the future.

The second "Divine Connection" was with Francine Ward, author of *Esteemable Acts*. Francine, after meeting you, I had the courage to "walk through my fears." Thank you for your testimony. Thank you for your inspiration.

Covenant Worship Center, I haven't forgotten you. I am so proud of my church family. Thank you for creating an atmosphere of worship in the services so that I can bask in the presence of God!

I thank God for my pastor. Pastor K. R. Woods, I have so much respect for you. You are definitely a pastor sent and called by God. Thank you for preaching the word of God that brings true deliverance. Thank you for speaking blessings into my life. Thank you for every counseling session for me and my family. I know God sent us to the ministry of CWC. As always, my prayer is to make God, my family and you, as my pastor, proud of me. You have poured so much knowledge into me as a minister and my way of honoring you is to show the world that I have been given Godly instruction by the best!

Finally, a special thank you to my enemies for being my footstool. Thanks for taking me higher!

Introduction

One morning I was on the train on my way to work. At the next stop, a woman and her young son boarded the train. As she and her son walked past me, I noticed her son had a blanket wrapped around him. They didn't look like they were homeless but there was something strange about the little boy and the blanket.

There were no empty seats in the car so she and her son had to stand up. As the train departed the station, I saw her begin to cry. A lady walked up to her and asked her if she was all right. She began to cry harder. I wasn't close enough to hear the conversation but I knew what she had been through. She wasn't homeless. I was looking at a woman and child who had fled from their abuser.

Once I realized what was going on with the lady, I got on my cell phone and called an intercessor to pray. As I described the situation, I fought back tears of my own. I could relate to this woman. I felt her pain.

I prayed for her and her son from my seat. The little boy must have reflected on the painful situation that caused them to flee because all of a sudden, he burst into tears. At that point, I could no longer hold back my tears. It was obvious he was trying to be strong but the burden was too great for him.

I wanted so badly to talk to the lady but I didn't want to intrude. Finally, I reached my destination and prepared to exit the train. As the train prepared to stop, I moved closer to the lady and motioned to her to keep her head up. She smiled and nodded. To my surprise, she was exiting the train at my stop.

I took advantage of the opportunity to minister to her. She told me that she had been "going through" with her husband since 3 a.m. She had been praying and asking God for strength to get out of the relationship. She explained to me that she knew she needed to remove her eight-year-old son from the abusive environment. We cried together as I encouraged her. I told her that she was stronger than she realized and to ask God for guidance.

As we parted ways, I cried more for the strange lady and the little boy who was wrapped in the blanket. I cried because she was sad. I cried because the little boy was afraid. Or did I cry because I saw a reflection of myself?

1

Face The Facts

Drug addiction is a wide spread problem in our world today. Over 2.6 million people worldwide are classified as being drug dependent. While our society calls drug dependency an epidemic or simply stated, a wide-spread disease, drug dependency or addiction is actually a strong hold that Satan is using to lure souls to eternal damnation. How can that be true? Well, chemical dependence is a symptom of demonic possession. The drug controls the individual on drugs. The drug dictates when that person eats, sleeps, goes to work, stays home from work, and goes out in search of more drugs. The addict is no longer in control of their life. They are literally possessed by the drug demon! Yes a demon. Another word for a demon is a fiend or an evil spirit. The street name for this demon is "dope fiend."

Satan uses many devices to turn our minds from God and salvation. In this day, one of the stronger devices he is using is drug addiction. When one is consumed by such a powerful strong hold the person begins to feel like there is no hope. Some have tried many different forms of rehabilitation. Those who struggle with an addiction may have tried inpatient treatment facilities, outpatient facilities, detoxification facilities, counseling sessions, and group counseling, but all to no avail. Some have tried to go to church and change their surroundings but the drug demon still calls them. A person may be able to stay away from the drug scene for a while but then the demon visits them in their dreams and lures them back to their drug of choice. One can be sitting right in a church service and an urge or a craving hits them and they run back to the drug. They may move to another city or state to get away from the people they know who do drugs or sell drugs but the demon follows them and introduces them to new "friends" or new "fiends" and they end up right back on drugs. The crack was calling them or the pains in their body told them they needed more of the heroin and so they are off again on a binge to chase a high. They are trying to chase a high that they felt when they took the first hit of crack or that first shot of heroin. Satan's clutches are tightened around their lives because they are chasing a high that can never be caught. Many times that leads to the addict feeling like the addiction is too big even for God to handle. All the while they are doing exactly what Satan wants them to do, which is to think there is no hope. Possessed. Stuck. Caught up. No way out. No escape. Eternally chained to the drug demon.

How then do we deal with such a powerful strong hold? What do we do for our loved ones who we see losing all of their possessions to drugs? What do we do for our loved ones as we watch them slowly kill themselves? How do we remain sane when our loved ones are stealing from us and lying to us to get more and more drugs? What do we tell our children when their parent is missing in action and out on a drug binge? What do we tell our children when the drug dealer comes knocking at the door? How do we know when to remain in a marriage when the spouse is on drugs? What do we do when we pray and the situation stays the same? Does God hear us? Does God care? Who is praying for us while we pray for the addict? Why is God allowing this to happen to my family?

Sadly, these are just a fraction of the many questions that Christians today are forced to ask. No longer can we send someone home and tell him or her just to pray for husband, wife or child without educating him or her about how to cope with the issue of drug abuse. We must understand that there is an evil driving force that was once an issue of the world that has now infiltrated the church, and we have to address it head on.

The bible speaks prophetically about the epidemic we are faced with today. The Apostle John wrote about the seven seals in the book of Revelation. Seals one through five refer to military hostility, conflict and conquest, civil war, economic disorder, pestilence, murder, and persecutions. These tragic events are signs of Christ's second coming. **Luke 21:9-12:**

> **But when ye shall hear of wars and commotions, be not terrified: for these things must first come to pass; but the end is not by and by. Then said he unto them, Nation shall rise against nation, and kingdom against kingdom: And great earthquakes shall be in divers places, and famines, and pestilences; and fearful sights and great signs shall there be from heaven. But before all these, they shall lay their hands on you, and persecute you, delivering you up to the synagogues, and into prisons, being brought before kings and rulers for my name's sake.**

The sixth seal deals with a catastrophe that couldn't be depicted even the best of Hollywood films. **Revelation 6:12-17:**

> **And I beheld when he had opened the sixth seal, and, lo, there was a great earthquake; and the sun became black as sackcloth of hair, and the moon became as blood; And the stars of heaven fell unto the earth, even as a fig tree casteth her untimely figs, when she is shaken of a mighty wind. And the heaven departed as a scroll when it is rolled together; and every mountain and island were moved out of their places. And the kings of the earth, and the great men, and the rich men, and the chief captains, and the mighty men, and every bondman, and every free man, hid themselves in the dens and in the rocks of the mountains; And said to the mountains and rocks, Fall on us, and hide us from the face of him that sitteth on the throne, and from the wrath of the Lamb: For the great day of his wrath is come; and who shall be able to stand?**

The seventh seal is made up of the seven trumpet judgments. In the bible, trumpets are symbolic of warnings and calls to repentance. In chapter nine, the sixth trumpet is sounded. The purpose of sounding the trumpet was to send a warning of the terrible events that were occurring. **Revelation 9:13-19:**

> **And the sixth angel sounded, and I heard a voice from the four horns of the golden altar which is before God, Saying to the sixth angel which had the trumpet, Loose the four angels which are bound in the great river Euphrates. And the four angels were loosed, which were prepared for an hour, and a day, and a month, and a year, for to slay the third part of men. And the number of the army of the horsemen were two hundred thousand thousand: and I heard the number of them. And thus I saw the horses in the vision, and them that sat on them, having breastplates of fire, and of jacinth, and brimstone: and the heads of the horses were as the heads of lions; and out of their mouths issued fire and smoke and brimstone. By these three was the third part of men killed, by the fire, and by the smoke, and by the brimstone, which issued out of their mouths. For their power is in their mouth, and in their tails: for their tails were like unto serpents, and had heads, and with them they do hurt.**

Plagues were loosed and many were killed. However, there are others that weren't killed. They were given space to repent. Instead of taking advantage of God's grace, their hearts became hardened. **Revelation 9:20-21:**

> **And the rest of the men which were not killed by these plagues yet repented not of the works of their hands, that they should not worship devils, and idols of gold, and silver, and brass, and stone, and of wood: which neither can see, nor hear, nor walk: Neither repented they of their murders, nor of their *sorceries*, nor of their fornication, nor of their thefts.**

Verse 21 is John's recording of the drug epidemic we are faced with today. The word sorcery as referred to in this verse, comes from the Greek word, "pharmakeuo" which means, "to administer a drug or to use enchantments" **(Liddell and Scott. An Intermediate Greek-English Lexicon. Oxford. Clarendon Press. 1889.)**

The bible assures us that there is nothing new under the sun. I believe that there is nothing new under the sun or the Son, Jesus Christ. John saw the drug plague in the spirit realm. Sadly, we are experiencing his revelation today, even in the church.

It's important to understand that the struggles of our addicted loved ones have become our own trials. The foundation of some of our ministries have been built upon the prayer life that was developed as a result of that father, mother, husband or child who was or still may be on drugs. The pain of watching them destroy their life caused us to go on fast after fast and constantly visit our prayer closets. For some, the loved one was delivered from the addiction. For others, including myself, we came out of prayer not with our loved one being delivered from drugs but with a greater anointing of our own, more defined character, and knowledge of our purpose in life.

We have to deal with this issue by being honest with our family and ourselves. Although you may have never experimented with drugs personally, somehow the effects of the addict in your family has altered your lifestyle. It's very easy to become accustomed to the behavior of someone who does drugs over a period of time. Their actions may be predictable but the pain in your heart never goes away as you watch them constantly destroy themselves. Denying the obvious only causes more problems.

So how do we cope with a plague that has come to destroy our lives? Unfortunately there is no magic formula to make this problem go away. No matter how guilty you may feel as a result of the addict's continued use, I pray that you release that guilt. Unless you actually put the crack pipe into the hands of your loved one, you are not the blame. Children who use drugs tend to blame their parents and husbands and wives tend to blame their spouses. The truth of the matter is anyone who makes the decision to experiment with drugs, use drugs socially, or turn to drugs as a means to deal with their problems only have themselves to blame.

If statistics report that 2.6 million people have been classified as drug dependent, I believe that it's safe to say that the number of family members being affected by their addiction is at least twice that amount. That simply comes out to at least one parent or one child who is adversely affected by the life of a drug addict. In actuality, most people who use drugs have *many* family members who are grieved by their use. Although there are millions of users, the number of family members who are crying and hurting over their use is probably closer to being in the billions.

At the risk of being insensitive to the struggles of an addict, I would like to point out that the addict has a very serious issue at hand. As previously stated, drug dependency is a powerful strong hold and a heavy burden to bear. However, everyone has a cross to bear. Sometimes we forget that we can't take someone else's problem and work through it for them. We can assist, encourage and support but we can't fix their drug addiction. As your loved one is fighting his or her battle with drugs, please don't allow yourself to get consumed and ultimately destroyed during their battle. After all, the only way you can truly be a help to someone else is if you are healthy in mind, body and spirit. So as you struggle with their struggle, remember that God is your strength and your guide. Allow the power of God, prayer and awareness of your own self worth lead and guide you into your healing and deliverance.

2

What Addiction?

"Whew! Another day at work has worn me out. That's okay because it's Friday and I'll order Chinese food, rent some movies and we can have a peaceful night. (Thirty minutes later) Now that dinner has been delivered we can wait a few minutes because Daddy will be home shortly. (Forty-five minutes later) Well, baby, let me fix you a plate now and you can start watching the movie but when Daddy gets home you'll have to rewind it back to the beginning. (An hour later) Yeah, sure you can have seconds but save some dried fried ribs for Daddy. (An hour and a half later) It's almost eight-thirty, where is he? When I talked to him earlier, he said he'd be right home after work. (Another hour later) I'll just put this food up and when he comes in, he can pop it in the microwave. Goodnight sweetheart, um, no, ah, I don't know where Daddy is. Ah, he said, that ah he would be here. Well, just go to bed and say your prayers baby. I'm sure he'll be home soon. I'll tell him to come kiss you when he gets in. I love you too dear." (In the bedroom, I hear the prayer of my four year old, "Lord, please send my Daddy home. In Jesus' name. Amen.") My heart sinks again.

It's 3:47 a.m. and the key is turning in the door. The stench of smoke and dope fills the air even before he enters the room. He's mumbling and grunting obscenities as he stumbles through the house. "Why did he come home if he's so miserable?" I whisper. "Better yet, what am I still doing here?" I ask myself next. Suddenly the bathroom door slams shut. The sound of an earlier meal and possibly some internal organs echoes through the walls as the toilet flushes. His dinner and my hopes of him getting off of drugs slowly spirals down the drain. I roll over once again feeling defeated and disgusted. Defeat because it seems my prayers weren't effective and dis-

gusted that I am married to a man who uses drugs. Humph! He doesn't think he has a problem!

How many people have you talked to that say, "What addiction?" when confronted about their drug use? Many times the user feels like their use is merely social. They feel like they are in control and really believe they have a handle on their use. Some may use drugs to mellow out after work. Some use to pick themselves up when they are feeling down or overwhelmed. It may have started with an occasional marijuana cigarette. The occasional use becomes a daily habit. Soon what seemed like a minor habit turns into a major addiction. Sadly, most people who are addicted to the "stronger" drugs like crack cocaine or heroin actually started out by socially smoking marijuana. As time goes on and their body becomes more dependent on that stimulant, they use more and more. Consequently, the effect of the drug becomes worse and worse. As their condition worsens, your relationship with them becomes more challenging.

The challenge arises when you realize that you are no longer dealing with your husband, father, sister or mother. Now you are dealing with a liar, a deceiver and a thief. On days when she's not using, you see your precious mother who brought you into this world. You see the one who nurtured you and encouraged you to be the successful person you are today. During the time when he is clean, you see your handsome father who taught you how to ride a bike. How could they have turned back to using drugs after being clean for so many years? Now the roles have reversed and you have to assume the role of the parent. You find yourself monitoring daily activities and confirming stories of where they say they are going or have been. This is not the way things are supposed to be. Instead of your mother coming to you for help to get off of drugs, she's coming to you for more money to continue to get high. When you tell her how much you love her and how much God loves her, and wants to help her, the only response you get is, "Don't worry about Mama, I'll be all right." For some reason, you believe her or maybe it's your own child who is on drugs. You want to help them and do all that you can to support them but the only support they really want is monetary support to fund their habit. Your son may look you right in the face and promise that he will pay you back this time, "for real." Your heart melts and you fall for his lie again.

How in the world can Mama be all right when you are looking at her wearing the same clothes she's had on for three days, smelling like she's been playing "*slip n slide*" at the city dump and scratching and twitching uncontrollably? If Junior is talking fast and sweating like he just ran a marathon but he has only walked from the crack house around the corner, why would you give him money? Junior wants to go get more drugs and Mama ain't all right! If they won't admit their problem, you can't ignore the obvious signs that there is a serious problem. Denial is deadly. Not only is it deadly for the user but also for the family and friends of the user.

It's time out for covering up for Mama, Daddy, Junior or Pookie. Stop telling people that Mama hasn't been to church for two months because she has been working. You know she lost her job three months ago for testing positive on the random drug test! Or you tell other family members that your sister Pookie is away on vacation. No, Pookie has been on a binge for the past two weeks and you really don't have a clue whether she's dead or alive. Now I know most people don't like to discuss their family members' drug addiction because they feel like that's "family business" or a "family problem." It's called an *Addiction*. It's an A-D-D-I-C-T-I-O-N! You'll find that people can't even say the word. When the user goes to rehabilitation or group counseling, they are encouraged to admit they have an addiction, but the family members remain in denial. They don't want the family look bad. Better yet, they don't want *their* image tarnished.

After all, it doesn't look good for Mrs. High Society to have a son addicted to crack. How can a minister's mother be a drug addict? Did you know that Prophetess Prayer Warrior's husband smoked dope? Baby, you'd be surprised at who is dealing with this very issue. Mothers who look like they have it all together are secretly grieving inside over their children's addiction. Fathers who are very prominent in ministry are aching at the thought of what their baby girls are doing out in the streets to get more drugs.

Don't let pride cause *you* to also say, "What Addiction?" If it's barking like a dog then it's a dog. If it's squealing like a pig, it's a pig! If it's mooing like a cow, it's a cow! If your money is coming up missing, the VCR, DVD and Playstation is gone, you have strangers coming to your door talking about outstanding debts or trying to sell you a yard broom at ten o'clock at night, then chances are, you are dealing with a drug addict! You saw it coming but you just didn't want to admit it. Now in retrospect, you look back six months prior and say, "Oh, that's why he made all of those trips to the ATM." "Oh, that's why he stayed out until 5:00 a.m." "Oh, that's why his job called looking for him." "Oh, that's why he became so important to other people (people you didn't know and have never heard of) and always had to take someone on an unexpected trip to the hospital at 2:00 a.m." Please! When the behavior changes and things are just too weird to be true, chances are, you are dealing with an addict.

You must be honest with yourself and the person struggling with the addiction. At some point you have to tell them flat out, "I know that you are on drugs but I love you and I'm praying for your deliverance." Stop pretending that your eyes are deceiving you. You are not ignorant. You are not naïve. You are not without discernment. God has been showing you all along that a problem exists but you have been denying it right along with the addict. Instead of praying, "God don't let what I think is going on be true," your prayer should be, "Lord, I thank you for confirming what I already suspected. Now help me to be strong and strengthen me to intercede on Mama's behalf." Just be honest with yourself. It doesn't make you a failure by admitting someone else's addiction, whether it's your parent, spouse or child. You haven't failed them. The decision to use drugs was their decision, not yours. Confronting the addiction head on is better than tiptoeing around the obvious.

It may be an admission that your family isn't perfect. That's okay. If you aren't comfortable talking to the lay members in your church, go to one of the ministers or the pastor and ask them to pray with you. If you are fortunate to belong to a ministry that offers support groups, I encourage you to go. Ask them to pray for your family member and for you as well. Let's face it, the pastor, the ministers and the congregation can pray for them but you are the one who has to live with or interact with them on a day-to-day basis. You need to be covered in prayer as you engage in this spiritual warfare on behalf of your loved one.

Your honesty about the addiction enables you to go to God in prayer with a clean conscience. **Hebrews 4:16, "Let us therefore come boldly unto the throne of grace, that we may obtain mercy, and find grace to help in time of need."** How can you approach the throne of grace seeking mercy and help for someone when you are lying and covering up the fact he or she is using again?

I know that it may be hard to think of an answer without giving up a lot of information when right after church one of the deacons asks, "Where is your wife? I haven't seen her in service in a while." There may have been times when asked those simple questions of concern that your expression displayed a look of bewilderment as if you were just asked, "What is the square root of 9,734,837?" Instead of saying, "Ah, uh, um, she's a, well, ah um she's fine," try simply saying, "You know Dec. Rubberband, she's having a really hard time right now and I sure would appreciate your prayers." That way, Dec. Rubberband isn't looking at you like you have been smoking something and you have requested someone else to go to God on behalf of Mama. The more saints praying for you and your family the better. **Matthew 18:19 says, "Again I say unto you, that if two of you shall agree on earth as touching any thing that they shall ask, it shall be done for them of my Father which is in heaven."**

The saints (not the people pretending to be a saved) aren't trying to be nosey when they ask about your family. That addiction can cause you to become so defensive when it's not even necessary. "Why is Dec.

Rubberband so nosey?" "Sis. Band-Aid is always trying to get in my business." "Why is Evang. Paperclip so concerned about my husband?" That's just the trick of the enemy trying to make you believe that the saints are against you. In actuality, the saints are genuinely concerned about your welfare. Many times God will use someone to ask the essential question to open the door for you so that you can ask for help. Satan will try to isolate you from your church family by having you think that your loyalty to your natural family means to keep quiet about the addiction. Dear heart, the truth of the matter is that Satan is setting you up to be a Co-Dependent.

3

Where Is God When I'm Hurting?

Dear God, my heart is so heavy today. It's been three days and I haven't heard from him. He promised that he wouldn't leave us like this again. I know that I shouldn't put my confidence in the flesh, but God, he's my husband. He's my covering and my protector right? Shouldn't I trust him? Shouldn't I believe him? I know the devil has been using him lately but he said that he would go to church with me and get saved. I saw him get prayer on Sunday and he even cried. I thought that was the breakthrough. The next day he was gone. When he came back home after a $500 binge, we cried together. He was so sorry and he promised that he didn't want to be this way. He asked me for prayer and I prayed for him and Lord I saw with my own eyes how you sobered him up from crack and caused him to be drunk in the spirit! I know that you are able to deliver because I saw it with my own eyes. I know that you are a righteous judge because I see the constant mercy you've extended to him.

I don't know why he won't surrender to you. Satan's power is not stronger than your power. God you are greater than any drug demon. Lord, I know it's a matter of his will to change. I want him to change but I realize that I can't change him. It's getting so hard to watch him deteriorate. He's lost so much weight. He doesn't even look the same anymore. He's not the man I married. He's not the man I fell in love with. What happened to him? What's so attractive out there in that lifestyle? It's so dirty and disgusting. How can he go days without showering or brushing his teeth? I know that he wasn't brought up like this. Where did he go wrong? Lord, will he ever make it back. What am I supposed to do in the meantime?

I don't know how much longer I can take this. Why does my husband have to be on drugs? Lord, I watch all of the other couples at church come to service together and leave together and they just look so happy. After church today, someone asked, "Where's your husband?" The only thing I could do was hold back the tears and shrug. God, it's so embarrassing when someone asks the whereabouts of your own husband and you can't answer them. The bad part about it is that most of the time I'm asked this question, I'm not trying to cover for him, and I really don't know the answer. Lord, your word says that you desire that I would prosper and be in good health, even as my soul prospers. Jesus, this isn't healthy for me. My heart is heavy and I feel a literal ache in my chest. I can't sleep. I'm worrying when I should be resting. I'm pacing the floor when I should be praying. My child is worried. He is learning how to put up a good front when company is around but when we are alone, he is crying his eyes out like me. I've been in pain so long, that I've become used to feeling this way. But Lord, now my baby is hurting. He doesn't understand why Daddy leaves for days at a time. I've run out of excuses. I had to finally tell him the truth. Now he is praying for his Daddy too. Lord, please help me! Please help us! Please deliver me! Please Jesus! Please show me what to do. Lord? Are you concerned? Jesus, can you hear me? Can you hear me now, Father? God, where are you?

I know that many of us have prayed this prayer so many times. I'm sure there have been countless prayer requests on behalf of drug addicted loved ones. At the same time, there have been just as many prayer requests for the families of drug addicts. Then there are those of us who went to God by ourselves and for ourselves asking Him for help with the burden that we were carrying. Isn't it something when you love someone how you carry their burden? It's as if you were more concerned about their life than they are themselves.

I believe it's because the spirit of God in us causes us to love them unconditionally. I know someone who uses the phrase, "I love you to death" quite often. I've taken that phrase and upgraded it to, "I love you beyond death." I realize as a child of God, I have a love for people beyond the grave. When I love someone, I don't want to just be in their life until death, I want to spend eternity with them. Since my objective is to go to heaven, I want all those I love and care about to go too! I want to see them saved so that we can spend eternity worshipping God together.

The love you have for your spouse, parent or child on drugs causes you to execute **Romans 15:1** that says, **"We then that are strong ought to bear the infirmities of the weak, and not to please ourselves."** When you really love them you take on their burden like the word of God says we ought to. However, in taking on their burden, you become weighted down with carrying your cross and theirs too!

So where is God when your heart is aching? Where is God when you are crying your eyes out after your husband has just sold his wedding ring for more drugs? Where is God when the drug dealer shows up at the door demanding payment? Where is God when you prayed that he would come home this time after payday and he didn't? Has God forsaken you? No dear heart, God has not forsaken you. **Hebrews 13:5, "…for he hath said, I will never leave thee, nor forsake thee."** God can't lie. He said that He would never leave us and He meant it. He is not a man that He should lie! He said in **Matthew 28:20 "..and, lo, I am with you alway, even unto the end of the world. Amen."**

Precious Heart, even during the loneliest hour, God is right there with you.

He was with the Hebrew boys in the fire. He is with you in your fire! He was with Daniel in the Lion's den. He is with you when you are hiding in your den away from the children crying uncontrollably. I know that there are times when you can't see God in the situation. Sometimes we can't feel God or hear from God. Sometimes God is silent when we ask Him questions. It seems like the more we seek, the more He hides. The prophet **Isaiah wrote, in 45:15, "thou art a God that hidest thyself."** But that doesn't mean that He isn't there. Keep asking Him for help. Keep asking your heavenly Father for strength. Keep asking Him for mercy. You are still here aren't you? Well, that means He has heard you and He is answering your prayers because He's kept you this far! There have been days when all I could do was pray, "Lord keep me." His loving kindness and tender mercies did just that.

As time goes on, you'll find that although the situation may be the same, through prayer, God has changed you. Mama may still be on drugs. Your husband may still be staying out all night. Your brother may still be stealing from you. Your sister may still be selling her body for more drugs. You may not have heard from your child in weeks. But God! He is still on the throne and He is still disbursing His ministering angels to cover you and to give you peace. You'll find your strength building up. I know it may be hard right now but He's building you. As you pray for the addict, He's building character in you. God is anointing you as you intercede for your loved one. Don't think that your prayers are in vain. While God is doing something for them, He's doing something for you. One morning you will have your Sudden Breakthrough! The day is coming soon when you will wake up with joy that you didn't know you had. Is Mama still on drugs? Yep! But God is still able! Is your husband still on crack? Yep! But it is well with my soul! The peace that surpasses all understanding will overtake you like Niagara Falls. When God sees that you are going to trust Him no matter what, He's going to give you peace. Right in the midst of the storm you will have peace. The peace comes when you realize I AM is in control of the storm. When you stop trying to work things out but give it over to I AM you'll have rest. **Exodus 3:14, "And God said unto Moses, I AM THAT I AM: and he said, This shalt thou say unto the children of Isreal, I AM hath sent me unto you."** When God says I AM THAT I AM, He's letting us know that He will become whatever we need Him to become when a crisis arises. God is saying, "Trust me because I AM your peace." When you acknowledge God and *totally* give your addicted loved one over to Him the blessings and peace will flow. Keep your mind on Him and He will keep you in perfect peace. That's His word!

I know the antagonist is still saying, "So where *is* God when I'm hurting?" Although we were taught not to answer a question with a question, I can't help but break the rules in this instance. Where are you *looking* for God when you are hurting? Where are you looking for God when you are going through? Where are you looking for God when the heartache is too much to bear? Let me give you a hint. Have you tried His presence? I mean really seeking God in prayer for help. It's good to pray and ask God for His presence. But have you tried asking God for His *manifest* presence. Make it personal. It's like knowing that someone is in the room because you know the scent of their cologne. Okay ladies, it's like knowing that *your* man is in the room because you know that cologne that smells oh so good on him! But his manifest presence is when you not only smell him, but when he comes over and oh so slightly pulls you close to him, takes you by the hand and lets everyone else in the room know that you belong to him! Hello! Yes Lawd! Now do you understand the point I'm trying to make?

I want to know that God is in the room but even more so, I want to feel Him pull me close and take possession of my issue! Thank you Jesus! I've experienced that ever so slight embrace from God during worship. His touch was so gentle that I didn't even realize that my wounded heart had been healed. All I knew was one day the pain was gone! The ache in my heart was no longer there. I was still concerned about my husband's addiction, but I no longer ached over it. That's when your name changes from "worrier" to "worshipper." When the true Lover of my soul touched me and took possession of my issue (only after I surrendered it because He's such a gentleman), I knew that everything would be all right. People may call you cold because to them you've stopped caring. It's not that you've stopped caring, but rather you've started caring about yourself and your children and you started caring enough to cast those cares that were driving you crazy on the altar so that I AM could work it out! Hallelujah!

You should strive to reach heaven with your praise. However, if want to invoke His manifest presence, I encourage you to try worship. If you worship God in the midst of the pain He has to show up. He has to answer. I know what it's like to lift your hands in total worship as the warm tears flow down your face. Those of us who have really been through something can relate to that feeling! It's the scene in church where you are just giving your all to God and your heart is heavy but you are crying out, "God I love you." It's the scene where the gossipers and the busybodies just know you have sinned because those tears are flowing way too constant! Ladies, it's the scene where you don't care that your make up is fading and running all over your beautiful suit because you just need to be in His presence. Gentlemen, it's the scene where you don't care about the snot running down your nose because you just need to tell your Father how much He means to you. Saints, it's the scene where God is smiling at you saying, "Now I'm getting glory out of my child."

God loves a worshipper. In fact He is looking for a worshipper. **John 4:23, "But the hour cometh, and now is, when the true worshippers shall worship the Father in spirit and in truth: for the Father seeketh such to worship him."** He loves a worshipper who will worship in the good times as well as the bad times. Worship invokes His manifest presence. When you are going through and you need a "quicker picker upper," get in His presence. In the presence of the Lord is fullness of joy and on His right hand are pleasures forever more! Confuse the devil the next time your loved one goes on a binge. Instead of getting upset, go into worship. Tell God how awesome He is. Tell God that He is worthy of all of the glory and honor. Tell God that there is none like Him. Tell God that He is mighty. Tell God that He is too wise to make a mistake. Tell God that you love Him for being in control. Tell God that you've never met anyone that could hold you together like Him. Tell Him that no one has ever touched your heart like He has. I mean just get intimate with God. Magnify Him! Make Him bigger than the fact that a binge demon has struck again. Glorify Him! Glorify Him in the face of the enemy. Just go into crazy worship and watch God move!

So instead of asking, "Where is God?" when you are caring the burden of someone else, start confessing "God Is." God is my help! When all of the money has been given to the dealer on the corner just begin to confess God is my Provider! When the drug dealer shows up at the door with threats, that is the perfect time to confess God is my Protector! When you don't know if she's going to come home tonight, that is a good time to confess God is my Comforter! The Almighty is Omnipresent. That means that He is everywhere. If God is awesome enough to be everywhere then He is awesome enough to be able to do anything but fail. All at once, He's able to strengthen me, comfort you and build up Sis. Peppermint who may live thousands of miles across the ocean. He is just that kind of God.

Satan desires to sift you as wheat. His mission is to get you off track. Don't let him trick you into backing up on your testimony. Discouragement can lead to sin. The enemy will have you thinking that God cannot or will not deliver your addicted loved one so you may as well give up too! The devil is a liar! God is not only able to deliver, but He is also willing. It's not His will that any should perish but that all would come to repentance. So it's not a matter of God's ability to save but rather a matter of your loved one's willingness to surrender and repent.

Precious soul, I want you to stay prayerful and encouraged. Continue to live for God. You should purpose in your heart to get back into the things of God. Go back to working for the Lord. Get that old notebook out and finish your book. Finish writing that song that would minister to the world about God's goodness. Stop denying your call and go back to preaching the word of God. Satan would have you to toss your gift aside. It's time to go to the spiritual lost and found and reclaim your ministry. While you are praying for the Lord to save someone else's life, I pray that God gives you the mind and desire to live your own life to the fullest.

4

Household Foes & Woes
(Journal Entries)

Matthew 10:36, "And a man's foes shall be they of his own house-hold."

Some of the most trying times of my life were experienced in my own home. Although my experiences were painful I am thankful today for every tribulation. Writing is very therapeutic for me. When my heart was heavy (which was quite often,) I put my feelings on paper.

In the following pages, I invite you to experience the emotional roller coaster I was on for a couple of years. There were days of happiness, sadness, relief and worry. When I look back over that period of my life, I know it was only God who brought me through the darkest hours.

Journal entry: 6/24/00

Today is our anniversary! Reservations are made for seven-thirty and we will have a wonderful dinner. Mom is going to baby-sit for us so that we can enjoy an evening out and then enjoy the rest of the evening in. We've had a rough year but by the grace of God, we made it to year number six.

"Baby is that you?" (pause) "What run do you have to make right now?" (pause) "Reservations are in an hour." (pause) "Right back!" (pause) "Why do you have to leave right now?" (pause) "Well, ok, just hurry back." (pause) "Ah, yes, we have dinner reservations for seven-thirty and it looks like we'll be a little late, do you have anything for eight? Even better, eight-fifteen will do. Thanks. See you then. Bye."

Eight-thirty comes and goes so I get in the car and go to dinner by myself. I cannot believe him! He's done it again! On our anniversary! He's not even trying! Here I am planning to spend a wonderful romantic evening with my man and he's off getting high again. How can he put drugs before me? He doesn't love me! I know he's had a problem but he saw how good I was looking when he left. I know he smelled my new perfume! Then he just leaves. He must be crazy. Does he think that I'm going to continue to take this? I am so sick and tired of him running in the house and coming up with an excuse to leave. Does he really think I believe him? I can't control him but I thought at least he would regard today as a special day and have mercy on a sista! I feel like I've been stood up at the altar on my wedding day. In retrospect, maybe that wouldn't have been so bad. I suspected something was up before we got married but I didn't want to believe it. Now six years into it, I love the man but I hate what he's doing to himself. Himself? I hate what he's doing to me! I hate what he's doing to our son! I hate drugs and everything associated with them! I see those little knuckleheads on the corner selling all of the time. If I see the activity why can't the police? I hate it that he's financing someone else's child to go to private school and now we can't even afford to send our own child. And who is this old guy he has been hanging out with lately? Why does he have to spend so much time at his house now? Why does he have to run his sister and mother all over the place now? When did he become their hero? I can't believe this man! As much as I have been there for him. I know I take good care of him at home! There's no need for him to wander. What's up? I'm sick and tired of this!

Journal entry: 7/28/00

I know we probably looked like a bunch of idiots, but desperate times call for desperate measures.

Today my cousins, my big brother, auntie and his mother had prayer in the house for him. He's been so out of control lately. We are all afraid for him. I don't know how a man his size can handle so much crack. He's not a big guy and doing drugs has caused him to lose weight even more. I hate what it's done to him. There's no more life in his eyes.

We prayed in the house and then anointed every room in the house. Some went out to the garage and prayed. Blessed oil was poured all around the house. I even poured it on the sidewalk in front of the house as I prayed. I know I looked stupid to the neighbors. I figured if he's bold enough to let them see him carrying all types of tools, equipment, and electronics out of the house to pawn then I would be bold enough to let them see me praying and pleading the blood over my family and house.

My heart is so heavy. Lord, please hear my prayer.

Journal entry: 8/10/00

Lord, please protect him! He called tonight and said that someone was holding him hostage, until he comes up with $100.00 that he owes them. I don't want to believe him but I don't know what to think.

God, I'm so scared. Please send your ministering angels of protection to help him get out of danger if that's really the case.

I can't take this! Why is this happening? I don't know if they are going to come here to the house. Lord, please protect us. Please cover us with your blood Jesus. Hide us from the enemy.

Lord this is too much!

Journal entry: 9/28/00

I have seen it all now! It's a wonder he doesn't get a hernia. Today he and some old looking guy with very thick glasses backed up the truck to the garage and loaded some huge piece of equipment on the truck.

When I asked him what he was doing, he said someone at the motorcycle club said it belonged to him and he was taking it to him. Yeah right!

If his dad could see how he's pawned off all of his tools and equipment in that garage, he'd roll over in his grave! He's been missing in action for two days and on the third day, he comes back hauling equipment to pawn so he can get high some more.

I don't even care anymore. I hope he never comes back!

Journal entry: 11/16/00

I've seen it all now! How do you pawn a truck? This man has gone and pawned his truck! I've heard people talk about smoking up everything they had but I didn't have a clue. I guess I'm seeing it first hand now.

We went on a little family excursion today to San Francisco. He gave them the truck. They gave him a few hundred dollars. We rode BART home and then he took off again.

Yeah, I see this is going nowhere fast. I hope this is his "rock bottom." He used to take pride in that truck. Now he has pawned it for money to get high. Maybe he'll realize how low he's stooped after he comes down from this high.

Journal entry: 11/30/00

Lord, I need you to help me! Help us Lord! Please show me what to do and how to help him.

Last night was so hard. He begged me for ten dollars. I kept refusing but he kept begging me for the money. This time he wasn't becoming violent. He just kept pleading and begging for the money. I told him that I knew he wanted to go get high with it so I wouldn't give it to him. I told him that I wasn't going to send my hard earned money to the crack house. He still kept begging.

I finally just took him in my arms as if he were a child and sternly told him, "No." He started crying and was still begging for the money. I stood my ground and didn't give in. I asked him what he would do with the money if I gave it to him. To my surprise he didn't lie. Shockingly, he came right out and admitted that he wanted to go get high!

We cried together as I held him in my arms on the living room floor. We fell asleep on the floor as I rocked him in my arms.

Lord please help my baby!

Journal entry: 3/19/01

Dear Baby,

I know we have gone down this road before, and I'm sure you can agree that it's tiring and not easy. It's hard to come to grips with the fact that we just don't understand one another and neither do we really understand each other's point of view.

You feel like I should know how much you love me because you "take care of me" so you say. I feel like you don't take care of me. Here are my reasons why. You have been blessed to receive a check every month for the past two and a half years that has afforded you the ability to take care of this home. Since you've stopped doing drugs every month, you have complained monthly about paying the mortgage and bills for the home and you had the means to do it. You say that I don't pay any bills towards the house but you are so wrong. You say that the family car is my car, yet it's available to you when you have needed it. Up until recently, you drove the car more than I did. You don't regard the car as our car, you say it's mine so by me paying the car note, you say I'm not contributing to the house. Then it's the issue of medical coverage. You still don't have your own medical coverage and I've had you covered for the past two years. But you don't regard that either. Up until last year, I've paid for private school so that our son could have a decent education. You don't regard that.

You say you love me but you don't even take pride in the fact that you can pay the bills for your family and you didn't even have to work to do it. I told you that I wanted to work with you and even prepared a budget to do so but you turned me down. Now you want me to give you money for the bills, but when I ask you if we could sit down together and write out the bills you refused that too. You are always threatening to put me out. You are always talking about getting rid of the house or signing it over to your family, but I'm supposed to feel like you love me.

Then there is the issue of your anger, bad temper and violent tendencies. I don't care how upset you get; you never have a right to threaten me. You are always talking about hurting me. But I'm supposed to believe that you love me. Then you tell me to get out. Then you tell me you don't want me to leave. Then you put it off on me and say that I don't love you. Baby, we can't function like this!

Then there's the issue of our son. You don't even support me in disciplining him. You hang out all hours of the night and then when you hear of an incident that has taken place, that I've already dealt with, you want to change the rules I've laid down. That's not right neither is it fair to me. He has to respect me and if you keep doing this he won't.

I know you love your son and I'll never take that from you. He loves you dearly as well. But we had a relationship before he came along and now it seems that it's over. Our relationship has dwindled down to nothing while you strive to get closer to him. You say to me that you don't want me to leave. But can you give me a reason why you want me to stay?

Journal entry: 4/3/01

It's been days and so much is in my head. Lord I'm just feasting off of the prayer last night. Thank you Lord for meeting us and blessing us in prayer. At the end of prayer, the Lord had me read Psalm 3. It says:

> A Psalm of David, when he fled from Absalom his son. LORD, how are they increased that trouble me! Many are they that rise up against me. Many there be which say of my soul, There is no help for him in God. Selah. But thou, O LORD, art a shield for me; my glory, and the lifter up of mine head. I cried unto the LORD with my voice, and he heard me out of his holy hill. Selah. I laid me down and slept; I awaked; for the LORD sustained me. I will not be afraid of ten thousands of people, that have set themselves against me round about. Arise, O LORD; save me, O my God: for thou hast smitten all mine enemies upon the cheek bone; thou hast broken the teeth of the ungodly.

Lord, I just thank you for the victory in the face of defeat! I can't imagine why people feel like there is nothing to calling on the name of the Lord. I know that the Prayer Service of most churches are the least attended services but I need this type of service! God I thank you for a time and place that I can come to call on you in prayer and supplication.

Later, when my bible just opened up to Psalm 37. It says:

> A Psalm of David. Fret not thyself because of evildoers, neither be thou envious against the workers of iniquity. For they shall soon be cut down like the grass, and wither as the green herb. Trust in the LORD, and do good; so shalt thou dwell in the land, and verily thou shalt be fed. Delight thyself also in the LORD; and he shall give thee the desires of thine heart. Commit thy way unto the LORD; trust also in him; and he shall bring it to pass. And he shall bring forth thy righteousness as the light, and thy judgment as the noonday. Rest in the LORD, and wait patiently for him: fret not thyself because of him who prospereth in his way, because of the man who bringeth wicked devices to pass. Cease from anger, and forsake wrath: fret not thyself in any wise to do evil. For evildoers shall be cut off: but those that wait upon the LORD, they shall inherit the earth. For yet a little while, and the wicked shall not

be: yea, thou shalt diligently consider his place, and it shall not be. But the meek shall inherit the earth; and shall delight themselves in the abundance of peace. The wicked plotteth against the just, and gnasheth upon him with his teeth. The Lord shall laugh at him: for he seeth that his day is coming. The wicked have drawn out the sword, and have bent their bow, to cast down the poor and needy, and to slay such as be of upright conversation. Their sword shall enter into their own heart, and their bows shall be broken. A little that a righteous man hath is better than the riches of many wicked. For the arms of the wicked shall be broken: but the LORD upholdeth the righteous. The LORD knoweth the days of the upright: and their inheritance shall be for ever. They shall not be ashamed in the evil time: and in the days of famine they shall be satisfied. But the wicked shall perish, and the enemies of the LORD shall be as the fat of lambs: they shall consume; into smoke shall they consume away. The wicked borroweth, and payeth not again: but the righteous sheweth mercy, and giveth. For such as be blessed of him shall inherit the earth; and they that be cursed of him shall be cut off. The steps of a good man are ordered by the LORD: and he delighteth in his way. Though he fall, he shall not be utterly cast down: for the LORD upholdeth him with his hand. I have been young, and now am old; yet have I not seen the righteous forsaken, nor his seed begging bread. He is ever merciful, and lendeth; and his seed is blessed. Depart from evil, and do good; and dwell for evermore. For the LORD loveth judgment, and forsaketh not his saints; they are preserved for ever: but the seed of the wicked shall be cut off. The righteous shall inherit the land, and dwell therein for ever. The mouth of the righteous speaketh wisdom, and his tongue talketh of judgment. The law of his God is in his heart; none of his steps shall slide. The wicked watcheth the righteous, and seeketh to slay him. The LORD will not leave him in his hand, nor condemn him when he is judged. Wait on the LORD, and keep his way, and he shall exalt thee to inherit the land: when the wicked are cut off, thou shalt see it. I have seen the wicked in great power, and spreading himself like a green bay tree. Yet he passed away, and, lo, he was not: yea, I sought him, but he could not be found. Mark the perfect man, and behold the upright: for the end of that man is peace. But the transgressors shall be destroyed together: the end of the wicked shall be cut off. But the salvation of the righteous is of the LORD: he is their strength in the time of trouble. And the LORD shall help them, and deliver them: he shall deliver them from the wicked, and save them, because they trust in him.

Lord, I just thank you for letting me know that you have my back!

Journal entry: 8/4/01

"Hello, it's me. I just wanted to tell you that I'm tired and I can't deal with this any longer. You said that you would stop using but you seem to be getting deeper involved. I don't like the example that you are setting for your son. If you won't get it together for yourself or for me, at least do it for him. This is not how it's supposed to be and I won't tolerate the lies, deceit and staying out late or not coming at home at all any longer. I want a divorce." Click!

Lord, I left him a message on his cell phone today telling him that I wanted a divorce. I know that you sent a Prophet to come minister to him, but I don't see him taking heed. I don't see the point of staying.

I know that my ways neither my thoughts are yours but I'm tired. I just feel like your love for me would cause the situation to change. I don't want to be married to a drug addict anymore. Neither do I want to be married to someone who has no ambition or drive to do more than hang out all of the time. He doesn't inspire me and I can't seem to inspire him.

What is the point of trying to be here for a man who won't even hear from you? He won't even return the calls from the pastor. It's like no one can get through to him. What does he need me for?

Journal entry: 8/26/01

Lord I thank you for the blessed weekend of rest I had at home with my family. It was truly a blessing to be home with my husband and son. The level of peace that is here today is just fabulous. God, I am so thankful. Thank you for meeting every need. You know the needs that we have and God by faith, I'm saying thank you in advance for every need being met.

I heard you tell me to fast today. You told me to fast for my strength in you. I also heard you say that I'm going to need strength for what I'm about to go through.

Lord, I don't want to go through another hard trial...

Journal entry: 8/28/01

Last night he hung out and came home after midnight. He had been doing something to get high. Smells like weed and alcohol. I dreamt that Auntie said that she had been praying for him. Today, when I called Auntie to see if she was going to follow up with him regarding the prayer that she prayed for him a few days prior, she said that she was in prayer about that decision. She said that she had been praying for him this morning because she felt in her spirit that he had went back out again. She said that she was waiting to hear from the Lord regarding the follow up.

You put Auntie on a fast and a consecration before you had her come to the house and minister directly to him about his addiction. You said through her, that you would perform the miracle in his life that day and remove the addiction if he wanted it done and if he believed. He was told to give up everything that day and not go back into another crack house or bar. You said if he did that he would lose. He was disobedient. He went back to everything he was told not to go back to.

Lord, it's scary living with him. It's like living with a walking time bomb. I don't like this feeling. I wish he would just get right and at least try to stay right.

Later on, Auntie said that the Lord released her from him. Lord have mercy…

Journal entry: 10/18/01

This man goes from one extreme to another. Now he's drinking heavily again. The stench of three or four Long Island Iced Teas is lingering throughout the house again. He doesn't even acknowledge how you cover and protect him. As much as he drinks and drives, it's a wonder he still has a driver's license.

He came in at 3 a.m. again. I'm supposed to just keep quiet and not say anything? Right! I feel like I have a right to question him but when I do he starts yelling at me. I can take the yelling but Lord he pushed me again. When he starts pushing me or grabbing my wrist, I just back off. Sometimes I get scared but Lord there were a few times I wanted to just go at it with him! But I feel like if I fight him back, I'll start cursing. If I start cursing and fighting, it might be easy for me to cheat on him again. I just started my preaching ministry and I'm not about to jeopardize my preach! I want to be anointed when I preach to your people. So please help me to endure the hardness as a good soldier.

Lord please keep me. Whatever you do, don't take your Holy Spirit from me…

Journal entry: 12/15/01

Church was off the hook today! It was just what I needed. It almost made me forget that I had been cursed out until 2 a.m. If the saints only knew how crazy my morning started! It was only the God in me that gave me the strength to pull it together to make it to church today. Thank God for a church that has a powerful worship service.

During praise and worship, I was able to just get lost in God's presence. I was able to bask in the sweet comfort of God's arms. I felt Him pull me close and heard Him say, "I'm here, come closer." The worship service was so high. The saints around me were so engrossed with being in His presence that they didn't even notice the dark circles or the bags under my eyes. Thankfully, we are accustomed to weeping in His presence so after church, after all of my make up had been wiped away with the tears, people probably thought my eyes were swollen from weeping in service and not from the three hours of midnight madness at home.

Lord, I'm exhausted. Please renew my strength.

Journal entry: 2/14/02

It's Valentine's Day and I'm in love with the Lord! I've also developed a new self love. I love myself so much that I'm going to make some changes in my life. God said that he wants me to be prosperous and in good health even as my soul prospers.

He has opened up a door for me to be free. I am scared because I don't know what's on the other side of the door. But by faith, I'm going to walk through it.

Thank you Lord for the changes that are coming in my life!

Journal entry: 02/20/02

It's been so peaceful the past few weeks. I can't explain the joy that I've been feeling. Looking back over the past few years, my soul truly does wonder, how I made it over!

Lord I thank you because I know that my trials really do come to make me strong. In the midst of the fire, it's been hard to see my way out but I thank you for proving yourself to me once again. Thank you for giving me the strength to go through even when I wanted to give up.

I heard you when you spoke to me today. Your voice was soft and still but I heard, "Kecia, it's not about you. It's not about him or the situation. It's about my glory." Thank you for choosing me and allowing a situation to come into my life where I can glorify you in spite of the pain. I'm glad that I've reached a level of maturity in you that when I'm faced with a trial, I run towards you instead of away from you like I used to do.

Lord, I could never make it without you. I wouldn't have made it this far without your grace.

5

My Broken Heart and Home

There were countless times I gave up in my mind. I didn't give up on the Lord but I gave up hope for the deliverance of my husband. After seeing him so messed up on crack, I just figured that I would someday be a widow. At the rate he was using, that someday seemed very close. The man I fell in love with was somewhere lost. Perhaps he was buried in the crack house. All I knew was the man I married was not the man I was now looking at. His eyes were so dark. His skin was dark and oily. His fingertips were raw from using his cigarette lighter and crack pipe for hours at a time. His hands were rough and his memory was gone. My husband looked like a dead man walking.

After a binge, he would often come home crying and begging for forgiveness. There were other times he would come home with a cocky attitude as if to say, "Yeah, I was out doing drugs and that's my business!" I was confused. I would be glad to see him home safe but then I wanted to kill him for making us hurt and worry about him. There were times I prayed that God would just take him. I figured he was killing himself anyway; why not just get it over with. He was losing weight and looking so badly. He kept drugs around the house and even did drugs in the bathroom. He put our son in jeopardy many times by allowing him to be around dealers or other users. Runners for dealers and dealers themselves came to our house to remind him of an outstanding debt and to demand payment. There was one time I answered the door with our son right by my side and a woman at the door asked for my husband. When I told her that he wasn't home, she said that some guy (a dealer) said that he had one hour to pay him his money.

I was afraid and furious. I hated the fact that he put us in situations like this. How could he say he loved us and allow us to be in danger? How could I continue to love him? My heart would literally ache from the pain that his addiction was causing our family. I just couldn't take it! I hated him! I wanted out! I prayed and cried. I cried and prayed. I pretended that I didn't care about him. I smiled when I went to work. I shouted and praised the Lord when I went to church. But my strength was wearing down. He wasn't getting any better.

My son was aware that Daddy had a problem but he loves his father and didn't want to be away from him. We have a very open relationship and finally I had to tell him the truth about Daddy. I was criticized for it but I couldn't avoid telling him the truth when he woke up day after day and Daddy wouldn't be home. Sometimes Daddy would go to the store and come back two days later. Other times Daddy would pick up strange people in the truck while he was with him. I felt like I had to be honest with him.

I told him how drugs are bad and people who sell drugs are bad. I explained to this four year old that drugs hurt people and their families. I refused to tip toe around the truth to give room for a generational curse to slip in! So that whatever choices he makes later in his own life, it won't be for lack of knowledge. He will know the truth and consequences of making the wrong decisions. I felt that it was my responsibility to instill in him what it means to live for the Lord. I taught him how to pray. He developed a prayer that he prayed dozens of times, "Lord, please send my Daddy home. In Jesus' Name. Amen."

We would be out at church or with family and my son would be fine. He would be full of life and enjoyed playing with the children and spending time with friends. As soon as we would get in the car to go home (just the two of us) he would ask, "Is Daddy going to be home?" Or he would say, "I hope Daddy is home." I know how much it hurts to watch your child began to worry about his father. It's as if all of the life and energy would be zapped out of him when we got in the car to go home. I was watching my child be consumed with stress over his father. Of course, I wouldn't know whether or not his father would be home so I would sometimes say, "Just pray." There would be times I would call before we came home to make sure his father would be at the house. At times he would be there so I would tell my son on the way home that Daddy would be at home when we got there. Sometimes he would still be there after I confirmed that he would be. Then there were other times even after I called he would be gone. It was hard to watch my son's face drop in disappointment. He would say, "But you said he would be here!" What could I do? There were times that when he would pray his little prayer, his father would almost instantly appear. When his father would come home, he would say "something" made him come home. I knew that God was honoring the prayer of a four year old.

One time, I decided to leave his father but the Lord dealt with me about leaving him because He hadn't released me. My son was miserable being away from his father. When the Lord instructed me to go back home to my husband, he didn't tell me things were going to get better. He just told me to be obedient. I was obedient and I went back home. Things didn't get better. Things almost seemed to get worse! We lost more money, vehicles, jewelry and trust to drugs. I didn't understand what was going on. I questioned God and asked him what was the meaning of this. The man wasn't trying to do right.

We moved our church membership to a church that is full of love and support from the pastor and wife to the greeters at the door. The excuse that "no one in the church understands" couldn't fly because there were men and women at our new church who had been delivered from the same addiction he was struggling with. There was strong Pastoral support and a strong men's ministry that was supportive but he wasn't ready to be delivered.

My self-esteem became low. I felt like his drug addiction was a result of me not praying enough. His mother accused me of being the cause of his drug addiction because we were having problems in our marriage. Excuses were constantly being made for his addiction. Was it the marriage? Was it his childhood? Was it his relationship with his mother? Was it his relationship with his father? Was it the death of his father? Was it child abuse? Was it a generational curse? I didn't know what the reasons were. Whatever the problem was or wherever the root of the problem existed, it made our lives a living hell.

He tried to change his eating habits to curb the craving for crack but it didn't help. He stopped drinking coffee because that would make him crave crack. He stopped eating chocolate because that would make him crave crack. The cabinet was stocked with vitamins and stress relief pills but it didn't help. He went to see a therapist but instead of the therapist helping, he would leave his appointments and go get high.

His addiction was so strong that a different pattern of his behavior had developed. I could read him like a book. I pretty much knew when he was about to take off. If I tried to encourage him to do the right thing and not leave, I would be accused of putting the thought in his head. He would go on a binge and once he returned, I was blamed for planting the thought in his mind to go get high.

During his two-year drug binge and quest for self-destruction, I was fighting hard to hold on to the Lord. I had just written the manuscript for my first book, *Return To Your First Love…A Plea To The Backslider.* Although no one had read the book, I knew what I had written. I had been through enough to know that I wanted to be saved and never leave the Lord again. My past failures and mistakes were so painful to my husband that the enemy convinced him that my past mistakes were valid reasons for him to go on binges. We both have tainted pasts. We both have made terrible mistakes in our lives. We both have had affairs. We both have broken the law. We would have shouting matches on who had the worst sins. We would have shouting matches on who committed the worst crime.

I was living for the Lord now and there was nothing I could do to change my past. I admitted the sins, repented, asked for forgiveness and suffered the consequences of my wrong doings. I still couldn't erase the past. I asked him to forgive me. I asked Jesus to forgive me but he kept saying that I was the blame for him being on drugs. I felt defeated. Nothing was being resolved. No changes were being made.

I didn't know how to love him past this problem. I began to condemn myself all over again for my past. I felt like I was failing my son as a mother for allowing him to be exposed to drugs by his own father. But I also felt guilty for wanting to take him away from his father. I became depressed and I believe that I was on the verge of a nervous breakdown. I had thoughts of suicide. One day I went on a rampage while he was out on a binge. I destroyed our wedding album and broke glasses from our wedding day. I had snapped! My life was consumed by an addiction and I had never even smoked the stuff. Several times, the enemy spoke to me and told me to get some crack and smoke it myself and let him see how it feels to have a wife on crack. That would have been crazy! We would have just been in the crack house together. Satan was trying to lure me out there by making me believe joining him would make him straighten up. Thank God for grace!

I was lonely and I was furious because he would be away on a binge and I would go right to the place he was staying and doing drugs. The people there always protected him because he was getting them high too. He became good friends with a guy who he smoked crack with. He stayed at the guy's house who had a sister addicted to heroin and a mother who was supposed to be a church mother but she was addicted to prescription drugs. (That's what he told me.) However, later I found out that he was having an affair with the sister who was a heroin addict.

She called our house for him one day. I came home early that day and as the phone rang, we both answered. I picked up the phone in the kitchen, and he picked up the phone in the garage. I heard her say, "I just called to tell you that I love you." His quick response was simply: "My wife" and she hung up the phone. I wanted to do some serious "laying on of hands" that day. I don't mean to heal either! That's why they were protecting him so much. They treated me as if I was intruding on them when I would come around looking for him. I was furious. First of all, he was cheating on me with a woman who lived with her mama. Secondly, she was a heroin addict! I feel like if you are going to take a risk to cheat on your spouse, make it worth getting caught. Why cheat with someone who is in a lower class than your spouse? I told him if he was going to mess up, he should have done better than that!

God is so good. A few weeks before I found out my husband was having an affair, the Lord directed me to, **Psalm 91:10, "There shall no evil befall thee, neither shall any plague come nigh thy dwelling."** Thankfully, God kept his word and I never contracted any diseases. I know because I was tested for everything!

I was crushed and I wanted to get back at him for hurting me. I considered having another affair but the Lord wouldn't let me go back into that lifestyle. Oh but I wanted to! I mean I really wanted to. I wanted to show him how to cheat. I wasn't going to go find something under a rock and mess up. If I was going to go to hell, I was going to go with a First Class ticket! Or if I had to go to go to confession, I was going to make it worth the trip. I wanted to get my groove back! I entertained the thought more than once. One occasion I had gone so far as to calling an old friend after I drove by the crack house and saw my husband's truck parked in front. When I made the call to set up the date, my friend said that he had just accepted overtime on his job. If I had gotten through five minutes sooner we could have hooked up. For some strange reason my cell phone was acting up and I had to dial a few times before the call went through. I mean I was trying to make that call but I couldn't get through! The Lord let me know that I had already asked Him to keep me and even when I got weak (I mean really weak), He honored my prayer and didn't allow me to fall back into sin.

The following Sunday, a guest speaker preached a message at our church about Christ being a "Bloody Road Block." She explained that the blood He shed on Calvary is still powerful enough to get us out of sin. The part of the sermon that stood out to me was when she said He would throw a monkey wrench in your plans when you plot to do wrong. That was my first experience with a "rhema" word. Yes indeed, that word was just for me and I received it. I knew that as long as I remained married to him regardless of his issues, I had to be faithful to him. But I still didn't know what to do about my situation.

I watched my son continue to love his father. The Lord told me that I could learn a lot from my child. He said to take note of how this child unconditionally loved his father. No matter how hurt he was and how long his father stayed away, he still gave his dad a big hug and told him that he loved him when he did come home. Taking note of my son's unconditional love helped me with my anger towards his father and the hate that I was starting to feel towards him. I was still hurt to see this child giving his father unconditional love when his father in return constantly abandoned him for drugs.

One day I came to understand **Matthew 10:36 that says, "And a man's foes shall be they of his own household."** I realized that I couldn't allow my husband's lifestyle cause me to lose focus on my walk with God. No matter what was going on with him, I had to be faithful to God. I was feeling faint but I was still determined to strive towards God. While I was striving in one direction, my husband was striving in the opposite direction. I wanted to live for Jesus and with His help, I was going to make it. However, taking this stand caused our spirits to be at war.

There were times he lashed out at me and said that I wasn't saved. These were times that that I knew I was saved! I knew I was saved because there was something stronger than I on the inside that was keeping me from going crazy. The Lord had to work **Matthew 5:44** into me. **"But I say unto you, love your enemies, bless them that curse you, do good to them that hate you, and pray for them which despitefully use you, and persecute you."** Another scripture the Lord impressed in my spirit about how to cope with someone else's drug addiction is **Ephesians 6:10, "For we wrestle not against flesh and blood, but against principalities, against powers, against the rulers**

of the darkness of this world, against spiritual wickedness in high places."

That's why it's so important to stay strong in the Lord and in His word. To get through the hard times, we must put on the whole amour of God. Keep your loins girt about with truth for those times when the enemy will try to pull you down with guilt by bringing up your past failures. Hold on to the truth that you may have messed up but God has forgiven you and pulled you out of the mess. Position your breastplate of righteousness to guard your heart from the heartache that comes with seeing a loved one hooked on drugs. Keep your feet shod with the preparation of the gospel of peace so that your walk with God won't get shaky during those times when it seems all hope is gone. Above all, hold on to your shield of faith to be able to withstand all of the attacks that the enemy will bring through accusations, lies, and deceit. Don't forget your helmet of salvation to protect your mind from all of the stress and pressure that comes through worrying about how much more you can take. Finally, put on the sword of the Spirit, which is the word of God or the chief weapon to be used against Satan.

Yes you are in a battle right now. You are in a spiritual battle and the enemy is not playing. He is serious with his attacks and you have to be just as serious in your defense. If you are smart, you will be serious in your offense as well! Fight this battle with the word of God and prayer. This battle is in the invisible realm. With the word of God and your prayers you are ready to wage spiritual warfare. You are ready to fight against the satanic forces that come against you and your family. Claim your own peace of mind and deliverance and then intercede on behalf of your drug addicted loved one.

6

Love The Addict, Hate The Addiction

How is it possible to love the addict and hate the addiction? The only way I was able to love my husband was through prayer. He constantly accused me of not loving him but that wasn't true. There were times when I thought that I really hated him but I came to understand that it wasn't him I hated, it was the addiction that I hated. I hated his addiction with a passion. I hated the demon that controlled his mind and behavior. I hated the demon that possessed his thoughts. I hated the evil spirits that he entertained while out on binges. I hated to think of how he looked smoking a crack pipe.

It is possible to love a person without loving their ways. The bible says that we can be angry but we are not to sin. I found myself in situations in this relationship when I would be quite angry but was held by God's word not to act out my anger. So I found myself loving my husband but hating the spirit that was operating in him. I figured if God can look beyond my faults and see my needs, I could do the same for him. I could love my husband but I decided not to remain a co-dependent of his addiction. I stopped giving in to his requests for money. I learned how to say no to him. The Lord sharpened my discernment and showed me how and when to support him financially. I had to devise a plan that wouldn't free up a lot of money to him, because the more I supported, the more extra money he would have for drugs.

It took a long time to get to the point where I could love him but hate his ways. At times, Satan had me feeling defeated when I reflected on how much praying I did for him and my family. I prayed, fasted, and cried about the situation for years. I prayed at home, at church, in the homes of family and friends for the Lord to deliver my husband and our family from this drug addiction. Contrary to what the addict may believe, their addiction affects the entire family. The long-term affects are emotional and financial. It seemed like the more I prayed, the worse he became. There were times when the drug binges slowed down. The binges became months apart instead of days and weeks apart. Whenever that would happen, I just knew this was it! The miracle was beginning to manifest.

One of the last binges I recall was when he had gone out and smoked about five hundred dollars worth of crack. I knew the dollar amount because I monitored his trips to the ATM. That was my way of knowing whether or not he was still alive. Every other hour, I would call the bank to see what transactions had transpired. He was getting sixty dollars here, one hundred dollars there, two hundred dollars on another trip. Since he could only withdraw up to three hundred dollars per day, I thought the binge would end if he reached his limit before midnight. When he wasn't home around 3 a.m., I would check the bank again, and sure enough, more transactions would take place after midnight. He would go on like this until he was tired or until there was no more money. It was usually when there was no more money.

This particular time, he came home and he went through his "I'm sorry" routine. He hadn't used in a while so he really felt bad that he had started up again. He was crying and begging for my forgiveness, but I wasn't buying it. I was cold towards him and told him that I just didn't want to hear anything he had to say. I told him to just go and shower because the smell of dope on him was disgusting. He showered and came back in the bedroom still crying. He got on his knees and asked God to help him. My attitude was, "Now you want Jesus." I continued to ignore him and he continued to pray. Then he asked me to pray with him. I responded with "What for?" I was tired of praying with him and for him only to watch him go right back out and do the same thing. Then he said, "How can you pray for all of those people at church who keep coming to the altar for prayer and you won't even pray for your own husband?" Man! He had me on a technicality! I was trying to figure out how could someone as high as he was at that moment be able to think so rationally. It had to be God. It had to be that familiar spirit in him that remembered that he once knew God. It had to be that cry of a backslider saying, "Someone, please help me get back to God."

Since he called me on the fact that I am an Altar Worker, I became an Altar Worker right in our bedroom. I got out the blessed oil and anointed my hands. I knew that I had to be protected from those demonic spirits that he had been entertaining. Then I anointed his head and asked him what he wanted from the Lord. He said that he wanted to be free from the drug addiction. I laid my hands on him and began to pray. I called out those demons in the name of Jesus! As I prayed he began to call on Jesus for himself. He asked God to forgive him and to save him. The power of God came into our bedroom as if we were in the middle of a Sunday morning worship service. I began to pray in my heavenly language so the devil couldn't intercept my request. All of a sudden at just about midnight, the bands were loosed, the shackles came off and my husband was sitting on the side of the bed speaking in tongues! I was so amazed at God that I needed a witness. I called my brother who lived around the corner from me to come over and see what God was doing. He arrived within five minutes and confirmed the move of God. He continued to encourage him and prayed with my husband more. We knew it was God because he began to repent to my brother for things he said to him in the past and for causing pain to me and to the rest of the family while he was on drugs. He continued to pray and sob on the side of the bed in nothing but his boxers!

This was it! This was the miracle that I had been waiting for. God is awesome. He can take a man who was high off of five hundred dollars worth of crack and sober him up and have him worshipping and repenting on the side of the bed in his underwear. My God is off the hook! I couldn't wait to see what was ahead for our lives. At that point I was convinced that a brighter future for us was ahead.

After that "upper room" experience in our bedroom, I believed in the miracle working power of God even more. I watched the man I love excited about the Lord. It was such a blessing to finally see him turn into the man I knew God wanted him to be. I was happy for him because I know how wonderful life is when you live for the Lord. Church folk often say, "Your worst day in the church is still better than your best day in the world." I was thankful that my husband now had godly help to go through every trial in his life.

I knew God really made a change in his life because he began to do things differently. He came straight home from work. That was something he hadn't done in a long time. He would come home and tell me how he had to drive home on a different street or take a totally different route so that he wouldn't be tempted to stop at his old hangouts. He told me there were times when people would try to flag him down but he would speed up and keep driving. Most likely, the people who were flagging him down were people he used to get high with.

There were mornings when we were getting dressed for church and he would be watching Dr. Creflo Dollar on television and I would be watching Bishop T.D. Jakes on television in another room. We would share the sermons we heard with one another and talk about how it blessed us or applied to our lives. One morning he asked me if it was normal to cry when watching sermons on television. I told him God's word was just as effective on television as it was in person and that if he cried when he heard the word, it was definitely normal for a saint. The spirit of God was making his heart tender and his was responding to His word. I was so thankful for the changes in his life.

Studies show that people with addictive behavior fall prey to various different vices. I have witnessed what these studies determined. While my husband was no longer using drugs, he struggled with cigarettes. At first he tried to cover up the fact that he started smoking again. He would chew gum or eat strong mints to try to mask the smell of cigarettes. I don't know why people who smoke think gum or mints can hide the scent of cigarette smoke on their breath. Not only could I smell the cigarette smoke on his breath but I could also smell it in his clothes.

I was beginning to worry because I knew if he started smoking again, he would eventually start doing drugs again. My worries were confirmed. I knew that he could be changed if he really wanted a change. The power of God is real but he had to walk in his own deliverance and have faith that a change was made in his life. **2 Corinthians 5:17, "Therefore if any man be in Christ, he is a new creature: old things are passed away; behold, all things are become new."** I guess he didn't have faith to believe and stand on God's word. I couldn't have faith for him. I tried to encourage him in the word. When I saw the biblical encouragement didn't work, I suggested he try one of those over the counter products to help him break his nicotine addiction. I know that God doesn't need any assistance with deliverance but if he couldn't have faith, I thought he should try one of those products if he really wanted to break the habit. People talk about getting saved and eventually getting set free from smoking cigarettes. I never read that in the bible. When you really submit to God, even deliverance from cigarettes is possible. Contrary to what some think, real saints don't smoke!

Eventually, he stopped hiding the fact that he was smoking cigarettes again. He would openly smoke on the front porch (at least he respected us and didn't smoke in the house.) It was pretty embarrassing to know the neighbors watched him smoke on the porch and then come inside and get all suited up for church.

Once he started smoking cigarettes again, eventually he started smoking marijuana again too. He once told me that smoking marijuana helped him fight the cravings for crack cocaine. Sadly, some people really think smoking a joint is better than smoking crack. People have said to me, "I may smoke my weed but I don't do that other stuff." A drug addiction is a drug addiction and to think that one drug is better or safer than another is ridiculous. Not only is it ridiculous, but it is just another tactic Satan uses to keep people bound to the tormenting force of the drug demon. Instead of using a joint to curb the crack craving, I suggested he try prayer.

Over time the cigarettes and marijuana use turned into heavy alcohol consumption. I knew he used to drink heavily before but he wasn't doing crack at the time. When he was using crack, he stopped drinking. So the vicious cycle continued. The more he drank, the more he stayed away from home. He was beginning to stay out later and later. Some nights he didn't even come home.

My heart was crushed to see the beautiful transformation destroyed by addiction again. I knew God was greater than Satan's grips on him. I didn't understand why he returned. Watching him return to that lifestyle gave me clarity that a person has to want to be delivered and stay delivered for themselves.

I learned how to discern his behavior. I knew the difference between a marijuana high and a crack cocaine high. I knew the difference between a crack cocaine high and an alcohol high. Although I loved him, I couldn't tolerate him entertaining demonic spirits. I hated to see him overtaken in his addiction but it got to a point where there was really nothing I could do for him except to pray.

He stopped coming to church. He began to accuse me of trying to make him be my "puppet" because I wanted him to go to church. I didn't want him to just go to church; I wanted him to go to God to get help. Once again, I watched Satan use the man I love.

He went from being verbally abusive when he used crack to being physically abusive when he drank. The alcohol brought out very violent rages. It took a long time for me to admit that I was a victim of domestic violence. There were times when I had bruises all over my body. Of course, my face was never bruised because that would have been too obvious. At the time, I only saw the bruises as an indication that he had too much to drink and not that I was being physically abused.

One year, around the time of our anniversary, I was planning a weekend get away. I went over to a close friend's house and was asking her for suggestions of where to go. How silly she must have thought I was to ask her about a romantic getaway when I had just showed her bruises on my shoulders and arms that he had recently given me! We never did go on that getaway.

It became clear to me that no amount of affection or sex for that matter could cure the demons he was struggling with. I learned that I couldn't love that demon away from him. My love for him looked beyond his faults and made excuses for his behavior, even when it was physically painful for me. No matter what, I couldn't love him to the point he would trust God for salvation.

I found confirmation in God's word. **Romans 13:10, "Love worketh no ill to his neighbor: therefore love is the fulfilling of the law."** That verse basically means that love does no harm. I still hung in there for a while longer even after God showed me His word. It was only after I endured a few more physical attacks that I said, "Enough!" I believe the Lord released me a lot sooner but my own fears paralyzed me into staying.

7

The Struggles of Co-Dependency

Wake up son. Wake up. Here let me wrap this blanket around you. Here just lie down in the back seat and go back to sleep. The car will be warm in a minute. I'm sorry I know it's cold baby. Momma is sorry that she has you out at two o'clock in the morning.

Where is he? I'm so sick of this. It's 2 a.m. and he's out getting high again. Where is that street? There it is. Now let me see his truck out here. It better not be down there at this crack house. It better not be. There it is! I knew it! He makes me sick. He said he was coming straight home from work today and now he's back at the dope house. I know he's not going to work.

Lord, I need you to help my mind. Last night, I took my baby out in the middle of the night to look for his father again. I was driving around like I was looking for drugs. I found his truck and I knew he was in that house again. The only reason I didn't get out is because my baby was in the car. I just sat in front of the house mad. I was hoping he came out but he never did.

I saw a police car parked down the street, so I drove up to the car. I went up to the officer's car and told him my husband was in a crack house using drugs. I begged the officer to go in to get him, but he wouldn't. He said something about having to get a call about a disturbance in order to go into the house. I guess my life wasn't a disturbance enough for him.

This is really driving me crazy. Lord if you don't help me, I'm going to lose it.

One day I made a Divine connection with a lady who has a beautiful spirit. Francine Ward, author of *Esteemable Acts,* challenged me to "walk through my fears." I took the challenge and decided to write the *Co-Dependency* chapter and include it in this book. The excuses I made to myself for not writing about co-dependency was that the subject was too clinical. I convinced myself I wasn't qualified to tackle this subject matter. After meeting Francine, I admitted to myself that I was afraid. I wasn't afraid to admit that I was a co-dependent, but I was afraid to address the issues surrounding my co-dependency.

> Terry Kellogg and Marvel Harrison wrote a book called, *Finding Balance...12 Priorities For Interdependence and Joyful Living* (Published by Health Communications, Inc.) They write, "Co-dependency is not about a relationship with an addict, but it is the absence of relationship with self. The avoidance may come from the fear of over-involvement, the fear of intimacy, the fear of abandonment or the fear of losing too much of oneself in a relationship."
>
> They further write, "Independence is the opposite side of the coin of co-dependence. A person with co-dependency may adopt a posture of independence. A person who isolates from relationships is in as much pain as a person who becomes lost in relationships. In reaction to co-dependence many people become counterdependent, defiant, or rebellious against authority, against intimacy, against law, and against their own dependency needs. They reject dependency in themselves and others. Counterdependence is a more aggressive posture than independence, and involves a battle with self in a system that creates more chaos and isolation. Sometimes counterdependence is necessary to break out of the repression of being over-controlled. Adolescents, for example, become counterdependent because their curiosity, creativity or being has been repressed or abusively controlled. It is a reactive co-dependent posture because it does not create true identity and facilitate integration and boundary development. Counterdependence can be a posture of power, but it is not self-empowering and tends to destroy the power of others. Much acting out can be thought of as counterdependence.

Co-dependency occurs in dysfunctional families, families with addiction, neglect, abandonment, abuse, victimization, dishonesty, unpredictability and denial and it affects all levels of our society.

Children who are abused, hurt, and neglected tend to continue this pattern, not just toward themselves, their relationships and their children, but toward their physical environment as well. Children who have been hurt will hurt their surroundings."

Being married to a man with an alcohol and chemical dependency was one thing, but when I became addicted to the drama surrounding his addiction, I realized that I had a serious problem. I spent countless days and nights worrying whether or not he was out doing drugs. There were times I couldn't focus on my duties at work because I would call him every hour on the hour to check his status. I would panic if the phone rang more than three times. If he would answer, I would carefully listen to the tone of his voice because I had become an expert on how to listen for the sound of a high in his voice. I could tell if he was using drugs by his tone, his conversation or how eager he was to get me off of the phone.

I would be afraid of him leaving my sight. If he went to the store, I would be a nervous wreck until he came back if he bothered to come back at all. I would worry as soon as he drove off but would be so relieved when he came back. The roller coaster ride that my emotions were on was very unhealthy. My life became consumed with worrying about where he was going, what he was doing, who he was hanging out with and how much he was neglecting his family. My prayers mostly consisted of petitions for him and protection and provision for all of us since he was putting us in dangerous situations and spending so much money on drugs.

It wasn't until I was writing this book that I discovered the root of my co-dependency. While I was married to my husband, the only way I saw myself ever being happy and free from *his* drug addiction was if God instantly delivered him and took the desire, taste and cravings for drugs from him or if he died. Those were the only two options I saw for my deliverance from his addiction. Only recently did I realize that I remained in an unhealthy relationship out of fear. I hated the situation I was in but I was afraid to walk away from it. The thought of being happy and surviving outside of that adverse environment was unimaginable to me. It's ironic how fear can paralyze you into staying in a relationship that is causing you so much pain.

I didn't always make the right choices in my life but I knew that I wasn't a bad person. There were times I felt like I was suffering from the consequences of my past mistakes. Were my sins so awful that God could and did forgive me but wouldn't forget what I had done? Was my past the reason I was suffering so badly in my marriage and in my home? Had I already been forgiven but didn't have the courage to walk in my forgiveness? Since the word of God is clear on forgiveness, sanctification through Jesus Christ and God's memory, the answer is clear why I stayed in an abusive relationship. I stayed because of my lack of courage to walk in God's forgiveness. **Hebrews 10:10-17** brings healing:

> **By the which will we are sanctified through the offering of the body of Jesus Christ once *for all*. And every priest standeth daily ministering and offering oftentimes the same sacrifices, which can never take away sins: But this man, after he had offered one sacrifice for sins for ever, sat down on the right hand of God; From henceforth expecting till his enemies be made his footstool. For by one offering he hath perfected for ever them that are sanctified. *Whereof* the Holy Ghost also is a witness to us: for after that he had said before, This *is* the covenant that I will make with them after those days, saith the Lord, I will put my laws into their hearts, and in their minds will I write them; And their sins and iniquities will I remember no more.**

Why did I tolerate the drug abuse? Why did I tolerate the alcoholism? Why did I tolerate the verbal, emotional and eventually the physical abuse? I tolerated it because at the time, I believed if you loved someone, you stayed with them and supported them until the end. The problem was that I didn't understand what the end meant. Since we were married, I thought the end of his addiction was the beginning of my happiness.

The dismal atmosphere of my home was a direct correlation of what I witnessed in my childhood. I knew that my husband could be delivered from drugs instantly because I saw what God did for my own mother. Over twenty years ago, my mother was addicted to cocaine. She was using drugs during the time snorting cocaine was more common than smoking it in the rock form with a pipe. It was during the time it was considered a party or social drug.

I remember when people would come over to our house and would always go into the kitchen to sit at the glass kitchen table. The grown ups always went into the kitchen and closed the door. They weren't eating dinner but they would sit at the table. I would be right on the other side of the door in the living room watching television. I don't remember any of their conversations, but I remember hearing a lot of sniffing. For a long time I didn't realize the sniffing was actually the snorting of cocaine.

Those were the days when cocaine was snorted in lines. There were always razor blades around the house. Razor blades were used to cut the drugs and divide it into lines. If Mom wasn't doing lines in the kitchen with friends and some family, she had a plate with lines of cocaine in her bedroom. By the grace of God she was able to keep her job throughout her addiction, but she worked odd hours and a lot of times my brother and I were left home alone.

One time I was at home by myself and I saw a plate of cocaine lines sitting on her dresser. I was inquisitive and wondered what the white powder the grown ups enjoyed so much tasted like. I figured if they spent that much time enjoying it, it had to taste good. I saw them licking the playing cards they used to snort with so it had to have some sort of flavor. So I walked up to the plate of lines, dabbed my finger in the white powder and licked my finger. It didn't have a taste to me so I went outside to play. When I reflect back on that day, I am so thankful to God. I used to love to play dress up in my mother's clothes and shoes. My cousin and I used to mimic my mother and her girlfriends and pretend we were smoking Virginia Slim cigarettes and planning to go out to a party. What if I decided to pretend to be Mom sniffing the white powder? My mother would have come home to her eight year old daughter dead of a cocaine overdose.

It was probably a year later when I read a book for the first time about drugs. I got the book from the library at my school. I remember sitting on the couch in our living room crying as I read the book because the book said that you would die if you used drugs. I was crying because I knew that my mother used drugs and I thought that she was going to die. I was afraid to let my mother see that I was reading a book about drugs so I hid it from her. Although I knew that she was on drugs, I didn't tell her that I knew.

I don't remember the effects the drugs had on my mother. She kept her job, we had food to eat and our lives seemed as normal as the rest of the kids in the neighborhood. She was as loving and nurturing to us as she could be as she battled with her own demons. I loved my Mommy. I loved her presence and especially her touch. It was always something about her touch that brought me comfort. Whether it was a touch on my forehead to check my temperature when I didn't feel well or when she held my hand, it was a special feeling. When Mommy was around, my fragile nerves were at ease.

I didn't understand the pain she was feeling inside. I didn't understand why she was using drugs. I didn't understand her need to go out and party to escape the realities of her world. The only thing that was obvious to me was I was terrified when I woke up in the middle of the night and she'd be gone. My heart would race, as I would wander through the house looking for her. It didn't seem to bother my big brother when she would leave in the middle of the night but it always frightened me. I would feel so empty and alone. She would always come back home but the fact that she was there when I went to sleep and gone when I awakened during the night, made me feel betrayed. It was like I was the parent and she was the teenager sneaking out at night.

We joke about it now, but there was this one time she went out and it was storming. The storm must have awakened me and of course, I was scared. So I called my grandmother who lived a good fifteen-minute walk away. I told Granny that Mom wasn't home and that I was really scared. I must have been crying because she made my dear Uncle Wendell walk in the storm at midnight to come to my rescue. Uncle Wendell had to fight the wind and the rain to come to his oldest niece's rescue. In fact, I was his only niece at the time. When he got to our house he knocked, banged on the door and called out our names but got no answer. Uncle Wendell had to walk back home in the rain because I had fallen back to sleep. The reason I fell back to sleep was because the thought of someone coming to my rescue was comforting and I was able to relax and fall back to sleep. Uncle Wendell never lets me or my mother forget that one! That story is funny today but those were the days my fears of abandonment were developed.

The first time I told my mother I knew about her drug use was the night she recommitted her life to God. It was a Sunday night and some young people were getting baptized. When I looked around, my Mom was praising the Lord and speaking in tongues. I was so happy that I started crying. I wasn't saved yet, but I knew if Mom got saved, she wouldn't be using drugs anymore! Immediately after the service, I hugged her with tears in my eyes and said, "I knew about the drugs." I don't even remember her response but I do remember that my little heart was relieved of the secret fear I had been living with.

My mother never used drugs again. If God could work a miracle in my mother's life without rehab or a twelve-step program, surely He could do it for my husband. I knew God was able so I expected my own deliverance from my husband's addiction to come the way my mother's deliverance came, which was instantly. For many years, I waited for that special service that would be so powerful that he would surrender all to God right then and there. I waited and waited for my miracle. I thought my miracle was going to be a change in his life. I received a miracle when my mom stopped doing drugs so I was looking for another miracle through my husband. That miracle never happened.

If he wasn't going to stop using drugs by his own volition, through rehab or the help of God, I feared the only other way for me to be delivered from his addiction was through his death. My father battled with alcoholism. Not only did he battle with alcoholism but his ultimate mistake was to run from his purpose. He ran from God's plan for his life. He ran to his early death. He ran away from me.

My father was a gorgeous man. He was a tall man with a big heart full of a lot of spirit. He was loveable when he was happy. He was terrifying when he was angry. As with my mother, I didn't know or understand the demons my father was battling with at the time. My parents were divorced when I was seven years old. He lived in another city about three hours away from us. Daddy didn't live with us so it was always mind boggling to be awakened in the middle of the night to sounds of my mother screaming and her cries for help. What could she have possibly done to upset him so much for him to come to our house and beat on her? She was so much smaller than he was. He was six feet three inches tall and she was five feet three inches tall. She was probably half his weight but he beat her like she was a man.

I loved my father but I was terrified of him. Since I was a kid, I didn't understand what triggered his anger. I just saw the result of it. My mother loved him dearly. It must have been her love for him; her insecurities and his charm that made her open the door for him to come into our house to beat her. Maybe he promised that he wouldn't hurt her again. Maybe he told her that he only wanted to talk. Maybe he used my brother and me as a tool to get inside. Whatever tricks or threats he used, he always seemed to come into our lives with an unexpected rage. However, there were times I can recall being around him when things were pleasant. Those memories are very scarce. I know that my heart would be glad when my daddy was in a good mood and happy. I would be so proud of him because he was handsome and tall. I would look up to him until he became violent. His violence towards my mother was so frightening that I remember my little teeth chattering and heart pounding with fear.

The last conversation I remember having with my father was on my eighth birthday. He teased me about being eighty instead of eight. The next year, he was dead. It was reported as a car accident. He had been drinking and was angry about something when he took off driving in his truck. He drove down some familiar roads in his hometown. Somehow, he drove into a ditch and his truck turned over. He died and left this earth without giving his life to God. He died and left this earth without becoming the preacher he should have become. He died leaving us fatherless. He left me.

Recently I realized that I equated my own happiness around my husband's problems with problems that my parents had. I saw that if you give your life to God even if you used drugs, God could deliver you instantly. On the other hand, I saw that if you ran from God, it could be dangerous and could lead to death. I wanted my husband to be saved and set free just like my mother. I knew that there was a call on his life. I had dreams of him preaching the word of God. My emotions ran high every church service he came to because I wanted him to be delivered. I wanted our home to be set free. I wanted to be happy. When he continued in that lifestyle, I would be disappointed that any day I would end up a widow. I was more afraid of him leaving me through death than of him leaving me for another woman.

It took a long time but I finally came to understand that my happiness was not based on him. It wasn't based on whether he stopped doing drugs or not. It wasn't based on my mother's life or my father's death. My happiness was up to me. I had to make a decision to be happy for myself, with myself and by myself. I had given so much in that relationship that I lost myself. I lost my sense of being. I lost my strength. I lost my drive. I became a frightened little girl again in a woman's body.

8

Destiny

I have a close friend who often says, "God won't override the will of man." Good and evil has been set before us. It is up to us to choose the path in which we want to take. God is patient and long suffering. He gives us space to repent. He is faithful and just. He gave you and I time to turn from our wicked ways and turn towards Him. He has afforded the same opportunities to our drug addicted loved ones.

Isaiah 55:6 says, "Seek ye the LORD while he may be found, call ye upon him while he is near." Sometimes people feel like they have stooped too low for God to help them. Another scripture written by the prophet **Isaiah is 59:1 that says, "Behold, the Lord's hand is not shortened, that it cannot save; neither his ear heavy, that it cannot hear."** God does still hear a sinner's prayer.

If you think about it, a drug addict hears from God. How many times have you heard your loved one say to you that they don't want to be an addict? How many times have you heard them say that they want to be saved? I believe that's a clear indication that they heard the voice of the Lord calling them. Perhaps it was something in their memory from many years ago in Sunday school that reminded them of God's saving grace. Perhaps it was the prayer of their mother, father or spouse that was beginning to activate conviction of their present condition that caused them to begin to think about giving their life to Christ. Many times instead of them running to God during those times of conviction, they run back to the crack house because of their own condemnation.

Whatever decisions they make in their lives, we must be confident that God is in control of our lives. We have to have enough faith to believe the word of God that says in **2 Peter 3:9, "The Lord is not slack concerning his promise, as some men count slackness; but is longsuffering to us-ward, not willing that any should perish, but that all should come to repentance."** The decision to change is their decision. Just like the decision to trust God for your protection, provision and sanity is yours. God's grace will carry you through the hard times. His grace is the glue that holds your heart in place although it feels like it's been shattered in a million pieces.

We don't always understand God's plan for our lives. I know I'm guilty of wanting to take a "peek" at God's divine blueprint concerning me. If I had believed that I could experience the peace and joy in God that I have now, I would have trusted Him *completely* a long time ago.

I realize that it was only God's grace that helped me to hold on during my lowest point. His grace is here for you too! During the time of the trial we can't see God's master plan but trust Him and know that there is purpose in your pain. **Romans 8:28, "And we know that all things work together for good to them that love God, to them who are the called according to his purpose."** God loves you and really does care about your situation. You may have to experience some painful times during your walk with God but I encourage you to keep walking.

The bible story of Joseph and his brothers is a perfect example of being hurt by family members. It was amazing how Joseph's destiny was revealed to him before his suffering took place. God showed him that he would be exalted and his brothers would bow to him. Some argue that he shouldn't have revealed his dreams to his family but his dreams were so awesome that he probably couldn't keep them to himself! Besides, who expects their own family to become so jealous of their dreams that they would try to destroy or even kill them? That's just something the average person doesn't even think about.

It's hard to imagine how our own flesh and blood could lie to us, deceive us and steal from us. I'm sure Joseph wondered the same thing while he was in his pit. His brothers lied on him, contemplated his murder, and stole his property. While he was in the pit, Joseph trusted what God revealed to him in the spirit. His family members threw him in the pit but God brought him out.

Joseph was a man who feared God and sought to please God. During the hard times, Joseph was faithful. He was faithful while he was in prison. Although false accusation landed him in prison, thanks to Sis. Potiphar, Joseph remained faithful to God. He resisted the advances of his master's wife because he didn't want to sin against God.

Joseph's faithfulness to God caused him to be promoted to second in command over Egypt. Due to a famine in the land, the same brothers who put Joseph in the pit had to come to Egypt where he was the governor to ask him for food. They were ashamed and afraid when they realized Joseph was alive and in charge. His compassion wouldn't allow him to be cruel or vengeful towards them. Instead he had mercy on them. Joseph was able to testify to them that God's divine plan included his suffering even by their hands.

I find myself relating to Joseph in a funny way. When I came back to the Lord after being away and outside of his will for some time, my attitude to serve Him was very different. I wanted to live for Him whole-heartedly instead of "straddling the fence" like I had done for so long in the past.

The Sunday I recommitted my life to God, my husband didn't come to church with me. He didn't understand how I could have gone to church, repented and committed to change my life without him. He knew the changes were coming. He knew that we would no longer be clubbing or partying together like we used to. Now, I didn't go to church, speak in tongues and come home and announce, "I'm saved now and things are going to be different!" I had to humble myself and respect my husband while still taking a stand for God. The trials were just starting.

Although I was going through an awkward adjustment at home with my husband, when I went to church, I praised God like I was going out of my mind! I had so much to be thankful for. I sang praises from the depth of my soul. I was studying the word of God and He was making His word so plain and clear to me. I was hungry to know the true nature of God. I searched the scriptures and prayed that God would reveal Himself to me even the more. I begin to find things in the bible I never knew existed. Weird things were beginning to happen to me that I couldn't explain. There would be times at work when I would hear myself talking about the word of God in my mind. It was so much being said, I would just begin to write it out. It was making me feel so good as I was writing it, that I wanted to just praise God at my desk! There were times when I would write the words on paper and it seemed as if my hand had a mind of it's own. The words were just flowing. I would write down some things and then I would walk to the bathroom and just pace the floor. Where was this stuff coming from? It wasn't very long after that when I realized that God had called me into ministry.

This was a really scary time for me. I felt like I needed to tell my husband that God was calling me into ministry. The night I told him, I was so amazed. We sat in the middle of our bed talking about the call on my life. I was crying and explaining to him that I was afraid of what people would say and think about me. The Lord used him to encourage me in a mighty way. If he never encouraged me again, he really encouraged me that night! He told me not to care or even think about what anyone said about my ministry. He told me to follow God and to forget about what anyone else said.

I took his encouragement and ran with it. The Lord used him to encourage me to go forth in ministry and the enemy used him to try to stop me from going forth in ministry. Like Joseph, I had a dream. I had an experience in the spirit realm that God revealed to me a long time ago. No matter what I had to endure, I knew the promises God had made me.

Hold on to the promises of God. Every trial and tribulation in your life has destiny written all over it. The painful part is the process. Sometimes the process will discourage you. It will have you to believe you didn't hear from God and that you will always be in the pit. Don't be fooled by Satan's tactics. **Genesis 50:20, "But as for you, ye thought evil against me; but God meant it unto good, to bring to pass, as it is this day, to save much people alive."** Satan doesn't realize that his pranks are preparing you for your promises.

The drug addiction demon didn't attack our home until after my husband encouraged me to go forth once I acknowledged my call to ministry. My greatest foe was in my own home. The enemy will use the closest person to you to keep you from your destiny. Again, don't be fooled! The woes and foes of my household pushed me deeper into the presence of God. The many days and nights of battling that drug addiction taught me spiritual warfare. The years of coping with that addiction taught me how to wait on the Lord and listen for His voice. Although this experience was very painful, I wouldn't trade it for the world. I'm glad God thought enough of me to allow me to go through this experience. **I Corinthians 10:13** gave me hope:

> **"There hath no temptation taken you but such as common to man: but God is faithful, who will not suffer you to be tempted above that ye are able: but will with the temptation also make a way to escape that ye may be able to bear it."**

God thought enough of you to give you this trial so trust that He's going to equip you with everything you need to endure. Loving the addict while hating the addiction is not an experience that you can simply go through without spiritual help or Kingdom access. Having access to the Kingdom of Heaven provided me with the comfort that I could make it in the midst of the storm.

> **Matthew 16:19, "And I will give unto thee the keys of the kingdom of heaven: and whatsoever thou shalt bind on earth shall**

be bound in heaven: and whatsoever thou shalt loose on earth shall be loosed in heaven."

As I reflect over this time of my life, I see how vital it was to have access to the Kingdom. When the drug dealer who was paying my husband crack to drive his heroin addicted wife to the methadone clinic came to me and asked me to baby sit their baby and I did it, I accessed Kingdom grace. I watched that little girl and Satan spoke to me and told me to hurt her because her father was hurting my family. The Holy Ghost told me to anoint her with oil and pray for her. That's when I accessed Kingdom prayer. About a year later, that same baby girl was caught in the midst of gunfire. Her heroin-addicted grandmother was shot in the head and chest while holding her in her arms but the little girl didn't get hurt. The Lord told me my prayer accessed Kingdom coverage. The Lord showed me how accessible Kingdom power was that time my husband came home from the five hundred dollar binge and went from being high on crack to drunk in the Spirit. However, when he chose to continue in that lifestyle God told me that I had endured enough and that I was released from the marriage. That's when I accessed Kingdom deliverance and freedom. He who the Son sets free is what? FREE INDEED!

Journal entry: Today

Lord I thank you for being good to me. You've shown me over and over again that you are a righteous judge. You've been good to my family over the years and I thank you for every trial that came our way.

I wish things could have worked out between us. I wish we could have stayed married. For many years I tried to stay by his side. I've prayed for him and with him but I know the decision to change is ultimately his.

Starting a new life is scary but I'm going to trust you. I just want to focus on working for you. Lord, I'm ready to be about my Father's business. If I can just work for you I'll be happy. I'm so thankful for the peace you've given me. I'm thankful that I no longer have to battle the drug and alcohol demon in my home. I hope that I can encourage at least one person to hold on to you in the rough times. I know that my purpose in this life is to encourage someone to stay strong in you no matter what.

I may not fully understand the strong hold of a drug addiction but I do know that the blood you shed on Calvary still has power to deliver today. I know that you can deliver people from drugs because you did it for some of my own family members. Maybe it's a matter of faith. Whatever it is, you are able to break any addiction Satan has to offer.

Lord, I know that you released me from that relationship but I pray that he returns to you soon. Although we are no longer married, he has a soul and I pray that his soul finds rest and peace in you.

Kecia

Conclusion

Spiritual Warfare

Ephesians 6:11

"Put on the whole armour of God, that ye may be able to stand against the wiles of the devil."

Spiritual warfare is the act of engaging in battle within the invisible spirit realm. The bible says in **Ephesians 6:12, "For we wrestle not against flesh and blood, but against principalities, against powers, against the rulers of the darkness of this world, against spiritual wickedness in high places."** We must remember that we are not fighting our loved one with a drug addiction but we are fighting the *spirit of drug addiction* that has them bound.

When engaging in spiritual warfare, you must pray to the Father in the name of Jesus. There is authority in the name of Jesus. Satan recognizes the name of Jesus. You also must have faith and believe that God is going to answer your prayer. Call those things that are not as though they were. It doesn't matter what the situation looks like, you must have faith when you pray. Since Satan is the accuser of the brethren, it's important for you to be in the right frame of mind and free from sin, hatred or unforgiveness before entering into spiritual warfare.

Worship is a powerful weapon to use when engaging in spiritual warfare. You can confuse Satan with your worship. When he sends his demons of depression, fear and unbelief to attack to, he will be expecting you to crumble under pressure but your worship will give you the strength to stand. Once you have gained the strength to stand strong through your worship, you can use your other weapon to totally annihilate the enemy. The other weapon is the word of God.

I encourage you to get to know this weapon very well. Anyone with military combat training, understands the importance of full weaponry knowledge. During a war is not the time to learn how to shoot a missile. Soldiers in the natural army spend years training and preparing to fight in a war. As soldiers in the army of the Lord, we should be just as vigilant in our training for spiritual warfare. We cannot afford to wait until the enemy attacks to learn how to use the word of God.

I have compiled some bible verses for you to study and memorize so that you will be prepared the next time the enemy comes to attack you and your family.

Scriptures for the battle:

<u>I Thessalonians 5:17</u>
Pray without ceasing.

<u>Ephesians 6:10-18</u>
Finally, my brethren, be strong in the Lord, and in the power of his might. Put on the whole armour of God, that ye may be able to stand against the wiles of the devil. For we wrestle not against flesh and blood, but against principalities, against powers, against the rulers of the darkness of this world, against spiritual wickedness in high places. Wherefore take unto you the whole armour of God, that ye may be able to withstand in the evil day, and having done all, to stand. Stand therefore, having your loins girt about with truth, and having on the breastplate of righteousness; And your feet shod with the preparation of the gospel of peace; Above all, taking the shield of faith, wherewith ye shall be able to quench all the fiery darts of the wicked. And take the helmet of salvation, and the sword of the Spirit, which is the word of God: Praying always with all prayer and supplication in the Spirit, and watching there-unto with all perseverance and supplication for all saints;

<u>Exodus 12:13</u>
And the blood shall be to you for a token upon the houses where ye are: and when I see the blood, I will pass over you, and the plague shall not be upon you to destroy you, when I smite the land of Egypt.

<u>Psalm 34:7</u>
The angel of the LORD encampeth round about them that fear him, and delivereth them.

<u>Isaiah 40:28-31</u>
Hast thou not known? hast thou not heard, that the everlasting God, the LORD, the Creator of the ends of the earth, fainteth not, neither is weary? there is no searching of his understanding. He

giveth power to the faint; and to them that have no might he increaseth strength. Even the youths shall faint and be weary, and the young men shall utterly fall: But they that wait upon the LORD shall renew their strength; they shall mount up with wings as eagles; they shall run, and not be weary; and they shall walk, and not faint.

Isaiah 43:1-2

But now thus saith the LORD that created thee, O Jacob, and he that formed thee, O Israel, Fear not: for I have redeemed thee, I have called thee by thy name; thou art mine.

When thou passest through the waters, I will be with thee; and through the rivers, they shall not overflow thee: when thou walkest through the fire, thou shalt not be burned; neither shall the flame kindle upon thee.

Isaiah 54:17

No weapon that is formed against thee shall prosper; and every tongue *that* shall rise against thee in judgment thou shalt condemn. This *is* the heritage of the servants of the LORD, and their righteousness *is* of me, saith the LORD.

Jeremiah 33:3

Call unto me, and I will answer thee, and shew thee great and mighty things, which thou knowest not.

Hebrews 1:13-14

But to which of the angels said he at any time, Sit on my right hand, until I make thine enemies thy footstool? Are they not all ministering spirits, sent forth to minister for them who shall be heirs of salvation?

Luke 11:10-13

For every one that asketh receiveth; and he that seeketh findeth; and to him that knocketh it shall be opened. If a son shall ask bread of any of you that is a father, will he give him a stone? or if *he ask* a fish, will he for a fish give him a serpent? Or if he shall ask an egg, will he offer him a scorpion? If ye then, being evil, know how to give good gifts unto your children: how much more shall *your* heavenly Father give the Holy Spirit to them that ask him?

John 14:13-14
And whatsoever ye shall ask in my name, that will I do, that the Father may be glorified in the Son. If ye shall ask any thing in my name, I will do *it*.

John 15:7
If ye abide in me, and my words abide in you, ye shall ask what ye will, and it shall be done unto you.

John 15:16
Ye have not chosen me, but I have chosen you, and ordained you, that ye should go and bring forth fruit, and *that* your fruit should remain: that whatsoever ye shall ask of the Father in my name, he may give it you.

Romans 8:18
For I reckon that the sufferings of this present time *are* not worthy *to be compared* with the glory which shall be revealed in us.

Romans 8:28
And we know that all things work together for good to them that love God, to them who are the called according to *his* purpose.

Romans 8:37-39
Nay, in all these things we are more than conquerors through him that loved us. For I am persuaded, that neither death, nor life, nor angels, nor principalities, nor powers, nor things present, nor things to come, Nor height, nor depth, nor any other creature, shall be able to separate us from the love of God, which is in Christ Jesus our Lord.

2 Corinthians 10:3-5

For though we walk in the flesh, we do not war after the flesh: (For the weapons of our warfare are not carnal, but mighty through God to the pulling down of strong holds;) Casting down imaginations, and every high thing that exalteth itself against the knowledge of God, and bringing into captivity every thought to the obedience of Christ;

An After Word of Prayer

Prayers of Petition

1 John 5:15
"And if we know that he hear us, whatsoever we ask, we know that we have the petitions that we desired of him."

Prayers of Petition

Prayer is a very powerful component to help you cope with the issues that come with dealing with a loved one with an addiction. Through prayer, God will give you strength to endure on those days when you feel like throwing your hands up in defeat. Prayer is also your access to the Kingdom of Heaven. I challenge you to develop a sincere prayer life.

Many times people outside of our homes may see a glimpse of our struggles and offer their suggestions or opinions about what you should do. However, through prayer and supplication, God will give you divine direction and guidance. During your time of struggles, I offer you prayer.

Prayer of Petition for Men

Father, in the name of Jesus, I pray for every father, husband, brother, and son who is hurting over the life of a loved one who is fighting a drug addiction. Lord I pray that you would give him strength to endure hardness as a good soldier.

Lift the burden and the heaviness of his heart. You said that you would never leave us neither forsake us and I ask you to remind the man of God that he is not alone even in this. Let every man find strength in your word. Let every man find strength in your arms. I pray that you give him a spirit of worship like never before. For we know that worship invokes your presence and in your presence is the fullness of joy! Restore joy and peace today, Father. Send your ministering angels to comfort my brother in the Lord. Let my brother know that it is okay to cry why the pain is great. Jesus, you wept so let my brother know he can weep too.

I thank you in advance for victory in his life. God I thank you in advance for deliverance in his family. Thank you in advance for giving my brother strength and wisdom to minister through word to that addicted loved one. I stand in agreement with my brother right now that no weapon formed against him or his family shall prosper!

We proclaim victory in the name of Jesus. Amen. So be it!

Prayers of Petition for Women

Heavenly Father, I pray for every mother, wife, sister and daughter who is hurting as she copes with a loved one on drugs. Lord, the women have been praying and interceding for the families, but I pray that you would strengthen them. Strengthen my sisters to continue to trust you. Strengthen her to continue to stand on your promises. You said that you would never leave her nor forsake her. So God I simply ask you to honor your word.

I pray that you would continue to be the lifter of her head during this hard trial. When the devil tries to discourage my sister with the realities of what her eyes may see, God I ask you to encourage her to walk by faith and not by sight. Give her wisdom to minister to and encourage her lost loved one. Let her words bring life and not death to the situation. Let her be wise to build her home and family and not tear it down.

Lord I pray that you would meet every need and teach her how to hide in the secret place in you. Teach her to trust you all the way and rest in your presence.

I stand in agreement with my sisters that victory belongs to her and her family. In Jesus name. Amen. So be it!

Prayers of Petition for Children

Dear Lord, I come to you on behalf of the precious children who are exposed to drug addiction by their parents. Lord, I pray that you would comfort their hearts and lift the burden that their little hearts are carrying.

Some children have actually witnessed their parents use drugs, but I pray that you would erase that scene from their precious minds. Cause them to remember the happier times in life. Even at their young age, Lord I pray that you would fill them with your Spirit. Teach them how to pray and seek you. Although the parent is supposed to be the responsible party, Lord I pray that these precious children learn how to call on your name for help. God, when they call on you, I pray that you will answer swiftly. Send your ministering angels to comfort, protect and provide for them.

Satan, I plead the blood of Jesus against you concerning our children. I break every generational curse that you would try to pass on to them. I cancel your assignment against them and declare that no weapon formed against them shall prosper. I pray healing for their mind, bodies, and emotions. In the mighty Name of Jesus. Amen. So be it!

Prayer for the Family Unit as a Whole

Father in the name of Jesus, I come to you asking for unity and peace for our families. Satan desires to sift us as wheat but we know that he is a liar. God, I pray that you would cause families all across this world to unite. Bind them closer together in unity and love. Let the love of Jesus Christ be the example that all families look to for strength.

Lord I pray that each husband be strengthened to be the head and love his wife and family as Christ loves the church. I pray that every wife submits to her husband and encourages him to be the man you have called him to be. I pray that the children are obedient to their parents as you have instructed in your word. Lord, bless every single parent in a special way. Let all of our families be full of love to ward off the tricks of the enemy. For those families that are suffering right now because of a loved ones drug addiction, I pray that you would give them strength, compassion and wisdom to cope with the problem until you bring forth deliverance. You are too wise to make a mistake. You are in control and I pray that their faith does not fail them during the hard times.

I declare that our families are made whole and healed by your love. In Jesus' name. Amen. So be it!

Resources

Resources For Drug Addiction

www.soberrecovery.com
www.al-anon-alateen.org
www.12stepforums.net/alanon.html
www.nasarecovery.com

Resources For Co-Dependents

www.codependents.org
www.allaboutcounseling.com/codependency.htm
http://skepdic.com/codepend.html
http://divorcesupport.about.com/cs/codependency

Resources For Alcohol Addiction

www.addictionalternative.net
www.healthrecovery.com
www.blackwomenshealth.com/Alcohol_Abuse.htm
www.naadac.org

Resources For Domestic Violence

www.domesticviolence.org
www.cpsdv.org
www.dtic.mil/domesticviolence
www.cpsdv.org

Made in the USA
San Bernardino, CA
16 November 2013